BECKY TIRABASSI

THE BURNING HEART CONTRACT

A 21-DAY CHALLENGE TO IGNITE YOUR PASSION AND FULFILL YOUR PURPOSE

INTEGRITY®
PUBLISHERS
Nashville

THE BURNING HEART CONTRACT

Published by Integrity Publishers, a division of Integrity Media, Inc.,
5250 Virginia Way, Suite 110, Brentwood, TN 37027.

HELPING PEOPLE WORLDWIDE EXPERIENCE *the* MANIFEST PRESENCE *of* GOD.

Cover and Interior Design by Susan Browne Design, Nashville, TN

ISBN 1-59145-281-3

Printed in Canada
05 06 07 08 09 TCP 9 8 7 6 5 4 3 2 1

CONTENTS

ACKNOWLEDGMENTS

I've been writing this book for almost thirty years . . .

I must begin by thanking my family—parents and siblings. Sometimes it is hard to be the relative of the author! But with each book I've written, I've grown to love and admire each of my family members as fellow sojourners in the walk of faith.

Of course, Roger, my husband, has been my best friend and wise counselor for almost thirty years. Most importantly, he has been my greatest encourager and trusted adviser in every area of life. My son has simply provided me with the best material! And as I write the final words of this book, I am witnessing a fresh wind of revival occurring in each of our lives . . . and it is wonderful!

My faithful co-workers and many friends have been extremely encouraging to me through the past few years, imploring me to write down this message that has been burning in my heart.

I must also thank just a few of my mentors: the Fellowship of the Burning Heart of 1947. Their example has lit a fire within me that has compelled me to fulfill the call in my life that I have waited to complete since the day I became a Christian, on August 26, 1976.

Because I am more comfortable as a speaker than a writer, I am deeply grateful for the exceptional editorial skills of my co-worker, Trisha Hubbs, who has truly allowed my passion for

acknowledgments

God to be captured in this book. Our editor, Jennifer Stair, has also been very careful and kind to allow my speaking style to be preserved within this book. My publisher has been patient; need I say more?

And I can't forget to thank the janitor, who stood by the door one day and spoke such life into my broken soul, mind, and body that I was instantly changed . . . I was powerfully filled . . . and I was given new life in Christ because he was not ashamed of the gospel. Thank you, Ralph.

Finally, if you are ready to be sold out, set apart, and sent out, I believe that *The Burning Heart Contract* will ignite a fire within you that can never be extinguished.

Your friend,
Becky Tirabassi

INTRODUCTION

The Gospel of Luke records an amazing story on the day of Christ's resurrection. Early Easter morning, Mary Magdalene and several other women rushed back to the disciples to report the shocking discovery of an empty tomb. The news rocked the community of believers who, just three days earlier, watched helplessly as the man whom they loved, followed, and believed was the Messiah died a horrible, violent death.

The same day, two of Jesus's stunned followers left Jerusalem and headed toward the village of Emmaus. Suddenly, Jesus Himself joined the men, but they did not recognize Him. As He talked with them, they seemed not to want Him to leave their presence. They begged Jesus to stay the night with them, and He agreed. When they sat down to eat, He blessed the bread, broke it, and handed it to the men.

The Bible says that at that moment, the men's eyes were opened and they realized who Jesus was. Then Jesus disappeared.

Suddenly *everything* made sense to the two men. They said, "Didn't our hearts burn within us as he talked with us on the road and explained the Scriptures to us?" (Luke 24:32). The two men quickly hurried back to Jerusalem to tell others about their encounter with the risen Lord.

Those with burning hearts walk with Christ, hear His voice, receive counsel and instruction, love Him deeply, believe in His holiness, and are passionate to share Him with others.

My desire is that this book will lead you on your own Burning Heart journey in which you encounter God in a new and powerful way.

If you want to possess an unquenchable passion to know God and make Him known, then each of the following stories, experiences, and challenges will set your heart on fire for God. I believe you cannot spend time in God's presence without being ignited in your own soul, so I pray that you will be met with a fresh touch of the Holy Spirit.

In this book, I will ask you to develop a personal Burning Heart Contract with God out of your own personal convictions and as a joyful response to who He is.

You will be asked to consider designing a written pledge detailing your personal convictions in light of God's Word on matters of your . . .

passion for God and willingness to spend time with Him daily,

pledge of purity to a holy lifestyle, and

pursuit of God's plan and purpose in your life.

I will give you options and suggestions on how you might write your contract to God, as well as examples of others who have written one.

Ultimately, the contents of your Burning Heart Contract will be your personal decision. I pray that your contract will reflect a lifelong commitment to be sold out, set apart, and sent out for the living, loving God.

PART ONE

WHAT IS A BURNING HEART?

It's painful for me to admit how desperately I craved love as a teenager. I always had lots of friends around me, and I tried to be the life of any party I attended. I doubt anyone recognized that my active social life was really an attempt to fill my need for acceptance, love, and attention, because we were all searching for the same thing. Like many, I hopped from relationship to relationship, trying to feel something significant. But by the time I was nineteen, I had been through a number of breakups, heartaches, rejection, and lonely days that left me feeling used and increasingly empty. I finally decided that the only way to solve my problem and find the love of my life was to leave Ohio.

No one was surprised when I dropped out of college at nineteen and announced that my girlfriends and I were moving to California. It just sounded like something I would do. I craved every drop of adventure that a new life in California promised—independence, parties, sunshine, blond surfers, no responsibility, and no rules. Most of all, I believed a fresh start in an exciting place (by Ohio standards) would bring me lasting love and happiness.

Soon after we reached the West Coast, I quickly set the

pace for my new life. I loved to dance and flirt and drink, so I went to bars every night, looking for adventure and that blond surfer I dreamed of meeting.

Unfortunately, all of my bad habits followed me from Ohio. In a very short time, I was totally dependent upon drugs, alcohol, and cigarettes; yet I was oblivious to the person I was becoming. I excused myself with the classic rationale that everyone was doing what I was doing. By the time I was twenty-one, I was smoking two packs of cigarettes a day, popping pills, filling the air around me with a constant spew of profanity, and drinking until I passed out or blacked out almost every single day.

It wasn't long before I met and moved in with a man who I thought loved me and would one day marry me. He didn't surf, but he was blond and that was close enough!

CHANGED BY LOVE

That next summer, a drunken incident changed my life forever.

I traveled back to my hometown in Ohio to be in a wedding. At the bachelorette party, after drinking half of a fifth of vodka with one other girl, I went home with a man I didn't know. I woke up next to him in the morning, concerned that I might be pregnant and humiliated that if so, I wouldn't know by whom. I was completely distraught.

No one had to tell me—I knew I was an alcoholic. If I had been sober, I would have never slept with this man.

I was disgusted with myself, ashamed, and scared that my

boyfriend would leave me. I was terrified to tell him what had happened. He was also on extended vacation at the time, so before he returned, I tried to stop drinking, clean up my act, and hope I wasn't pregnant. But during the long, excruciating wait, I began going through alcohol withdrawal and experiencing anxiety attacks. I went to the edge of sanity and emotional stability.

Then, as if perfectly timed either to throw me over the edge or to finally catch my attention, I received a notice requiring my appearance at a court hearing for a car accident I had caused one year earlier while drinking.

On the morning of August 26, 1976, I prepared to go before the judge and testify about the details of the accident, most of which were a complete blur. I desperately wanted to abandon my addicted, broken, morally loose life, but I had nowhere to turn.

Before we walked into the courtroom, my lawyer put his hand on my elbow and said, "Rebecca, if you lie on the stand, you'll be crucified." I had only heard of one person who died by crucifixion, and that was Jesus Christ. I had attended church every Sunday until I left home, and I thought I knew all about God and Jesus. Like most of us, I grew up singing "Jesus Loves Me," but as a young woman, I had no capacity to understand those words or believe they were true for me.

That morning, I clearly saw who and what I really was, and I believed there was no way I was lovable to God. Yet without realizing what was happening, God's voice was gently calling me to Him.

Immediately following the court hearing, I was filled with thoughts of suicide. But instead of taking my life, I drove straight from the courthouse to a church. I had to find someone with answers or help or hope. The only person in the building was the janitor of the church, who was buffing the floors of the children's classroom in the basement.

In my miniskirt and platform shoes, and through makeup-streaked sobs, I poured out the details of my desperate situation to the janitor—beginning with the bachelorette party and culminating with the court hearing. Though he clearly understood that I was possibly pregnant, addicted to drugs and alcohol, and uncertain how my boyfriend would react after hearing of my unfaithfulness, the janitor simply said, "Let's pray."

I remember thinking, *Okay . . . anything to get rid of this shame.*

In a simple prayer, he led me to ask God to forgive me, change me, and pour the Holy Spirit of the living God into my life.

I was desperate for love, but I never dreamed that God's love would grab hold of me in this way. I felt it gripping, changing, healing, and freeing me. I was aware that this love was unearned and certainly undeserved. God's overwhelming kindness drove me to my knees and then sent me soaring with sheer joy.

Even while I was praying, I could feel God's love sweeping through my heart. I was lit with a consuming passion that was bursting with flames. I couldn't fathom how this love had found me, yet I knew I couldn't let it go.

Something unexplainable—in human terms—happened that day. I experienced and received something invisible yet real. My transformation began with an emotion of love that swept over me, accompanied by the amazing relief of forgiveness. I was filled with the deep happiness that had eluded me for so long. In that moment, in that prayer, I found hope as I realized I had a second chance to start a new life.

FIRED UP!

Everything was different when I came out of the church basement that day, but not all of the adjustments were easy. Initially, I lived a divided existence between my old and new lives. Tugs toward the old life fueled feelings of anxiety, fear, shame, guilt, and powerlessness. Yet the draw toward the new life stretched me to recognize and pursue real love.

As a new believer, I was confronted with tempting situations around the clock. My friends pressured me to return to my old life and give up my newly expressed love for God. To them, the old Becky was a lot more fun! But because I was the one to cry aloud the words, "Come into me, Holy Spirit; change me, help me . . . If You don't save me, I cannot live another day," I remained resolved. I refused to turn back.

Previously, I couldn't muster an ounce of effort to change a habit, but now, because I knew God loved me, I began acting differently. It was as if I suddenly wanted to please Someone very special and make Him proud of me.

I quit swearing, even though my filthy mouth had an incredibly wicked reputation of its own. I simply refused to let a curse word cross my lips; it seemed like utterly unacceptable behavior after what I had just experienced.

And I was no longer willing to continue polluting my body with the substances that had controlled me for so long. I realize that most people who struggle with alcohol addiction don't instantly quit drinking in a day, especially after a seven-year binge—but I did. Many recovering alcoholics relapse and relapse and relapse—but, miraculously, I didn't.

Was it a healing or a miracle? This I know: it was an experience so real that I'd be a fool to turn my back on such unbelievable love.

I very much wanted my boyfriend to prove his love to me by asking me to marry him. But the very same day I prayed with the janitor, I walked into my apartment, looked around at the place I shared with my boyfriend, and knew I had to make arrangements—right away—to move out and live on my own. I hadn't heard a sermon or read a Bible verse about love or marriage, but I intuitively understood that God's love promised something more lasting, more secure, and more sacred for me.

Yes, God's love ignited a response from me so powerful that my actions, attitudes, and aspirations changed immediately. After a few short months, I moved back to my parents' home. The longer I maintained sobriety and sexual purity, the more I experienced a deep desire to know God better and to understand His purpose for my life.

I wanted everyone to know about God's love that had forever changed me! The first people that came to mind were students. I was such a lost, hungry-for-love teenager that once I found true love, I wanted others to experience it too.

My fire for God was contagious! Within a year, I became a full-time youth worker, and the following year, I married a fellow full-time youth worker. Our hearts for God and for each other were alive and passionate. I assumed I'd feel that way for the rest of my life!

A FADING FIRE

But over time, even though I had a dramatic, life-changing encounter with God, other priorities crept in and nearly extinguished my fire. Unintentionally, I had failed to tend the flame of my passion for God. In fact, I was unaware that it was even fading.

Though I didn't recognize the signs of a dimming fire, author O. Hallesby developed a list that perfectly described my life at that time. His indicators of a passionless believer include lack of prayer, more "world" in our thoughts, less "God talk" in our conversations with others, and a diminishing "sting" from sin.[1]

After eight years, a few cooling embers barely remained lit within me. By then, my devotion to God and my awareness of His presence and power upon my daily life was subtly replaced by other habits and commitments. I exchanged my time with God for time given to my husband and son, my volunteer work, watching television, and sleep. I allowed every other role and responsibility in my life to gradually gain more time in my schedule and thoughts.

I never officially decided to quit praying or talking to God; it just slowly happened. Without prayer, my life was out of touch with God and out of order! I was no longer consumed with God, fueled with courage, or expectant of miracles. Instead, I was consumed by anger and out-of-control appetites. I was critical and complaining, negative and hurtful to others, prayerless and hopeless.

Then I attended a yearly conference for youth workers. By the time I got to the convention, my passion and purpose were almost completely extinguished.

As each speaker called us to purity and prayer, I was awakened to the danger of becoming a passionless believer and an overworked leader who cut off my greatest source of fuel. I was done pretending; I broke down crying and finally admitted I needed to change. God met me that week and provided desperately needed instruction on how to reignite the fire within.

Most of us know what it's like to attend a conference and experience a boost of inspiration and determination . . . only to watch it dissolve within a few days after returning to the real world of jobs, families, and responsibilities. But at that convention, God lit a fire so strong and so real that it has not diminished in more than twenty years.

Each speaker that week talked about spending time—real

time, lots of time, dedicated time—in conversation with the living, loving God. They proposed the unthinkable! They suggested spiritual disciplines that gave past powerhouses of faith exactly what they needed to fuel their passion, overcome their weaknesses, find and fulfill their purpose, and ultimately impact countless thousands for the living, loving God. And though no one issued a specific call to do so, spending at least one hour a day in prayer like John Wesley, Martin Luther, and Bill Bright became my burning desire.

In any generation, people find it difficult to set aside time for prayer. But throughout the centuries, those who most changed the world for God proved that spending significant time in prayer is both possible and strategic.

Once I faced the truth about my prayer life, I was forced to agree with Leonard Ravenhill, who wrote, "Prayerlessness in the life of a believer is sin."[2] I was hurting God, my witness, my family, my future, and myself by neglecting to spend daily time with Him. Sure, I said quick prayers. Sure, I read my Bible right before I fell asleep. Sure, I prayed for people . . . if I remembered. But I had lost any discipline to set myself before God on a daily basis for any length of time.

Before I left that convention, I confessed my failure to spend time with God. In front of a woman who could hold me accountable, I vowed to spend at least one hour a day, for the rest of my life, with God.

FUEL FOR LIFE

I went home completely "on fire" to be a different woman. As I gave the Holy Spirit more control of my attitudes, actions, and appetites—He took it!

I pored through books by those who were masters of spending time with God and found great nuggets that were as practical as they were spiritual. Corrie ten Boom, a Holocaust survivor, once said, "Don't pray when you feel like it. Make an appointment with the King." So I did. This commitment was simple but profoundly life changing.

Though I was a busy youth worker, wife of a busy youth worker, mother of a toddler, coach, program director, and volunteer trainer, I began daily fulfilling my commitment to spend one hour a day talking and listening to God.

For a woman with many responsibilities and great need for God's power in my life, I could not justify my laziness, busyness, or sleepiness any longer. Especially as a person in spiritual leadership, I could not give God's life-changing and life-empowering love to others if I was not being filled and fueled.

Suddenly, I was compelled to *pray* more rather than *do* more! I was finally awakened by the pleas of writers such as Leonard Ravenhill, who wrote, "To be much for God we need to be much with God."[3]

And for more than twenty years, I have spent at least one hour a day with God. Not because anyone asked me or made me, but because God called me and because I need to be reignited, refueled, and recharged every single day to . . .

    live and

        love and

            believe and

                achieve beyond my own abilities!

To help me make the most of my hour with God and to keep myself from daydreaming or falling asleep, I asked God for an idea that would keep me accountable and organized. The idea He gave me more than twenty years ago was to develop a notebook that I still use to this day, and more than 250,000 others have used it as well. It's called *My Partner Prayer Notebook*, and it has two parts:

God's Part—where He talks to me through His Word,
    and
My Part—where I talk to Him in writing.[4]

I have boxes and boxes filled with two decades' worth of handwritten, two-way conversations with God. The pages are filled with my prayers to God and His responses to me received from daily Bible reading, His Holy Spirit, sermons, studies, or other messages.

In more than twenty years, I haven't grown bored of our meetings or too tired to meet with God! I welcome His counsel, because I know that no one loves me like He does. In these hours with God, I am both disciplined and encouraged. I receive ideas for myself and for others. Ultimately, I'm *still* so happy to be loved and heard and helped that sleeping in or not planning ahead for our time together simply aren't options.

I believe with all my heart that this hour of power is the place where . . .

> I receive daily fuel to keep my passion for God alive and burning,
>
> I am daily prompted to confess any sin in my life—in writing,
>
> I hear God's call to purity and holiness,
>
> I receive specific direction to fulfill His plans for me, and
>
> I am given courage to believe in the impossible!

AMAZED BY GOD

Many, many years after I made the decision to pray for an hour a day, I was inspired, and actually surprised, when I read the life story of Bill Bright in the book *Amazing Faith*.[5] Even though I had been an acquaintance of Bill and Vonette Bright for quite a few years, I had never heard about the contract he wrote and signed with other friends in 1947. Tucked away in the pages of Bright's book is the remarkable story of how a contract with God set the hearts of ordinary people on fire for God.

The development of this contract occurred during a weekend teacher training conference led by Henrietta Mears,

Sunday school teacher and mentor to hundreds of students at First Presbyterian Church in Hollywood.

One night during the retreat, Mears delivered a powerful message on being fully committed and "expendable" for Christ. Later in the evening, Bill felt compelled to go to Henrietta's study room to talk and pray. Two other men, Richard C. Halverson and Louis H. Evans Jr., felt similarly compelled, each on his own accord.

Without a plan or agenda, the informally assembled group of four was driven to their knees in prayer. They were overcome by God's presence calling them to reach the world, especially college students, with the love of God.

Anointed through a vibrant encounter with the Holy Spirit, their prayer time produced untamed enthusiasm for the gospel and a plan for reaching students for Christ. Before they went their separate ways that night, they initiated the Fellowship of the Burning Heart. And they recorded on paper the lifetime commitments they made for the purpose of giving themselves over entirely to the God they loved.

The significance of the signed contract represented a powerful turning point in each of their lives, yet oddly, it has received little public attention beyond the pages of Bright's biography.

The written contract read:

> I am committed to the principle that Christian discipleship is sustained solely by God alone through His

Spirit; that the abiding life of John 15 is His way of sustaining me. Therefore, I pledge myself to a disciplined devotional life in which I promise through prayer, Bible study, and devotional reading to give God not less than one continuous hour per day (Ps. 1).

I am committed to the principle that Christian Discipleship begins with Christian character. Therefore, I pledge myself to holy living that by a life of self-denial and self-discipline, I may emulate those Christlike qualities of chastity and virtue which will magnify the Lord (Phil. 1:20–21).

I am committed to the principle that Discipleship exercises itself principally in the winning of the lost to Christ. Therefore, I pledge myself to seek every possible opportunity to witness, and to witness at every possible opportunity, to the end that I may be responsible for bringing at least one to Christ every 12 months (Matt. 28:19; Acts 1:8).

I am committed to the principle that Christian Discipleship demands nothing less than absolute consecration to Christ. Therefore, I present my body a living sacrifice, utterly abandoned to God. By this commitment, I will that God's perfect will shall find complete expression in my life; and I offer myself in all sobriety to be expendable for Christ (Rom. 12:1–2; Phil 3:7–14).[6]

IGNITED BY PASSION, PURIFIED BY FIRE, ABLAZE WITH PURPOSE

Reading this four-point contract stopped me dead in my tracks. The straightforward principles in the contract were the very same convictions God had put on my heart decades earlier— commitments to prayer, purity, and purpose. I had always highly respected Bill Bright and Henrietta Mears for the work they accomplished for Christ during their lives, but now I had uncovered a tangible blueprint for their passion, purity, and purpose.

Their sold-out love for God and willingness to invite the Holy Spirit into every area of their lives enabled these four people to live above their weaknesses and beyond their limits. They committed to "absolute consecration to Christ," and none of them would ever be the same.

Consider how God was able to use the expendable lives of those who put their commitment to Him in writing that night:

- Bill Bright went on to found Campus Crusade for Christ, which is estimated to have led well over fifty million people to Christ around the world.

- Richard C. Halverson wrote twenty-six books and eventually became the chaplain of the United States Senate.

- Louis H. Evans Jr. authored a number of books and pastored churches around the country, including Bel Air

Presbyterian Church and National Presbyterian Church in Washington, D.C.

- Henrietta Mears was the director of Christian education at First Presbyterian Church in Hollywood for thirty-five years, founder of Gospel Light Publications and Forest Home Christian Conference Center, and co-founder of Gospel Literature International.

Even now, as I consider the vows that each of them made to God, I am most compelled by the realization that they were not prompted to make these commitments because of an outcry against a liberal culture or resistance to political correctness. Instead, a deeply profound experience with God ignited a passion within these four Christians that produced burning hearts for Him. It changed their lives and eternally impacted the lives of others for the living, loving God.

The first non-negotiable and most time-consuming tenet of the commitment they made that night was to spend one hour each day with God, talking to Him and listening to Him. As they spent time with God, they knew they could not help but be changed by His presence and purified by His Spirit. And their passion to share God with others became more contagious.

THE BURNING HEART CHALLENGE

In February 2002, I spoke at a convention for youth workers.

In the weeks leading up to the event, I was continually impressed with the thought that I should not give my favorite talk on prayer. Instead, I spent several days considering the power unleashed in the lives of Bill Bright and the others when they put it all on the line for God.

I felt led to call the roomful of overworked and underpaid youth workers to embrace a burning heart for God by making a commitment to spend one hour a day with Him. Additionally, I challenged them to commit to complete sobriety and purity and service to God.

A former member of my youth group, now a business owner, husband, and dad, attended the convention with me. When I issued the Burning Heart Challenge to kneel before God and answer the call to prayer, purity, and purpose, he did so! I'd known him almost twenty years at the time, and though he had a fabulous heart for ministry and a deep commitment to his family, his life has changed more in the past two years than in the first twenty years I knew him. He is bolder in his faith, is more committed to his time with God, and has humbly embraced a life of sobriety that has set him apart as a leader in a very loose culture.

As another year passed, my desire to share the Burning Heart Challenge with others—especially college students—increased. I couldn't seem to stop thinking about the millions of people who have been impacted by Bill Bright's life and ministry, or the four hundred people who were called into full-time ministry under Henrietta Mears's mentorship.

So, in October 2004, I issued another Burning Heart Challenge at a chapel service for students at Azusa Pacific University in Southern California. This time it felt like the roof was lifting off the place as the Holy Spirit broke powerfully into our gathering through my unscripted words and the students' response.

I told them I felt that God wanted me to share two stories with them. First, I shared the account of the day God miraculously saved and dramatically changed me, immediately calling me to sobriety, purity, and purpose. And second, I told them how God had called me to spend one hour a day with Him for the rest of my life.

Then I stood in front of the student body and said, "Society gives you all the permission you need to live on your terms. You don't need any more permission. But here's what I believe God wants me to call you to—holiness and purity."

"What would happen," I asked, "if you were an entire student body that left this place set apart and holy?"

Then I asked the students to stand or kneel or come forward to respond. I challenged them to spend one hour a day with God for the rest of their lives and to commit to a life of purity and holiness. For almost an hour, students stayed to pray and worship, to make tearful and public confessions, and to commit their whole lives to God.

Afterward, a woman on staff came to me and said, "In six years, we've never seen this kind of response after chapel."

I worried I was bringing a challenge that might be too

tough for most. But the Holy Spirit knew the students were ready. It seemed they were waiting for someone to call them to be sold out, set apart, and sent out.

A mother who had been at chapel e-mailed me from her daughter's computer: "Thank you for calling kids to purity and prayer." Another student e-mailed me and said, "Chapel changed my life."

I am absolutely convinced that hearts everywhere are longing to answer the call to deeper passion, purity, and purpose for God.

In the following pages, you will experience a twenty-one-day adventure designed to ignite your passion, purify you by fire, and set you ablaze with purpose. At the close of this book, you will be given instructions on how to develop your own Burning Heart Contract, which reflects your commitment to live the rest of your life sold out, set apart, and sent out for God.

PART TWO

A 21-DAY ADVENTURE IN PASSION, PURITY, AND PURPOSE

IGNITED BY PASSION

Bill Bright, Henrietta Mears, Louis H. Evans Jr., and Richard Halverson entered into the Fellowship of the Burning Heart in 1947 out of a response to the Holy Spirit of God drawing them into an extensive time of transparent confession and powerful prayer. The experience of being in God's presence ignited their deepest passions.

Compelled by their love for God, they understood that . . .

- keeping their hearts ablaze for God required being continually fueled with indomitable, inexhaustible, resourceful, impenetrable, and indispensable power;

- only the Word of God and Spirit of God could supply a man or woman with the supernatural power of God;

- in order to impact their world and make a difference with their lives, they could never let their very real love for God diminish;

- being the most effective, sold-out people they could be for God meant they could never ignore, resist, overlook, or become too busy to receive daily fuel. Otherwise, they risked depleting the source of their burning hearts for God.

Those with burning hearts passionately desire more of God: more of His Spirit, more of His Word, and more time with the One they love.

So it seems appropriate that the first non-negotiable and most time-consuming tenet of the Fellowship of the Burning Heart was a commitment to spend no less than one hour a day with God.

Your Burning Heart Contract will reflect your desire to know God better and to love Him more by spending time, *real time*, with Him. A passionate soul cannot exist independently from its source. If you long to live a vibrant, on-fire life, you must plug into the heart of God and let His love pierce you, change you, inspire you, and always draw you closer.

Prayer is, as Ros Rinker says, "a dialogue between two people who love each other."[1] I encourage you to let the Holy Spirit woo you more intimately into His presence during the next seven days. Draw near to God daily, hourly, moment by moment, so that His fire ignites your passion to know more of Him.

May these daily readings inspire you to open up consistently, instinctively, purposefully, naturally, and passionately with the living, loving God.

DAY 1:
STRUCK BY LOVE

It is truly amazing to consider how a tearful confession in a transparent conversation with the unseen God in front of a stranger could so dramatically—and almost instantly—change everything about me. Yet nearly thirty years later, I vividly recall the day, the hour, and the place when love changed my life. I was so deeply forgiven and so greatly loved that I still celebrate the anniversary of that day every year. One thing I understood then and still understand today is that God loves me just the way I am.

Whether you are new to the faith or a longtime believer, we all view God's love toward us with a limited human capacity to understand love. Today, I challenge you to open yourself to loving God with your whole heart . . . and to being loved by God just the way you are.

Recently, my pastor gave a sermon on a very familiar passage in the Bible—John 3:16, which says, "For God loved the world so much that he gave his one and only Son, so that everyone who believes in him will not perish but have eternal life." This verse is so familiar to most of us that we typically read right past it.

One of the interesting things about this verse is that it says God "loved" us, not "loves" us. This is significant, my pastor said, because the Greek usage of the little "d" on the end of the word means that God's love originated before time existed. In other words, there was nothing you or I could ever do, or will ever do, to earn or deserve God's love. God loved you and me before we were born. He loved us from before all time. He does not love us if or *because* we love Him; He loved us before we ever knew Him.

God's love toward us is both intentional and passionate. In Jeremiah 31:3, He says, "Long ago the Lord said . . . 'I have loved you, my people, with an everlasting love. With unfailing love I have drawn you to myself.'"

One of my favorite devotional books, *Streams in the Desert*, tells the powerful story of a Christian man who had never felt God's love in the way that others seemed to experience it. God's love had never overwhelmed him with emotion or compelled him to drop to his knees in tears and prayer.

Through the years he was a faithful church member and leader. And though he recognized his lack of a passion for the living, loving God, he continued to dutifully attend church meetings to know God better.

One night he encountered God in a most intimate and unusual way during an evening church service. Throughout the entire sermon, he kept waiting for a word that would move him in any special way, but the sermon ended and he felt nothing out of the ordinary. As the preacher closed with prayer, the man was preparing to leave without receiving what he'd come for when he heard the pastor say, "Oh Lord, Thou knowest we can trust the Man that died for us."

At that moment, the man knew he had received the message he was meant to hear. Later, as he took time to digest such a powerful statement, the impact of the preacher's words erupted in personal conviction and confession. He wrote:

> I rose and walked down the street to the train; and as I walked, I pondered deeply all that consecration might mean to my life and—I was afraid. And then, above the noise and clatter of the street traffic came to me the message: "You can trust the Man that died for you."
>
> I got into the train to ride homeward; and as I rode, I thought of the changes, the sacrifices, the disappointments which consecration might mean to me and—I was afraid.
>
> I reached home and sought my room, and there upon my knees I saw my past life. I had been a Christian, an officer in the church, a Sunday-school superintendent, but had never definitely yielded my life to God.
>
> Yet as I thought of the daring plans which might be baffled, of the cherished hopes to be surrendered, and the chosen profession which I might be called upon to abandon—I was afraid.

I did not see the better things God had for me, so my soul was shrinking back; and then for the last time, with a swift rush of convicting power, came to my innermost heart that searching message:

"My child, you can trust the Man that died for you. If you cannot trust Him whom can you trust?" That settled it for me, for in a flash I saw that the Man who so loved me as to die for me could be absolutely trusted with all the concerns of the life He had saved.[2]

In that day and hour, the man was struck by the experience of God's intentional love for him. Through one sentence at the end of a prayer, he was deeply impressed with the incredible sacrifice Jesus made for Him. He could only respond in one way: complete devotion for the rest of his life to the One who loved him.

The emotional and powerful ways in which we are personally struck by God's love are the defining moments that impact our lives forever. They are unique to us. They are meant for us to have and to hold. They might be as simple as a sentence in a prayer, a story in a sermon, a kind word from a stranger, a moving lyric, or an absolutely life-changing explosion of God's Spirit upon us through a miraculous series of events. But when a passion for God is ignited within you, you will be immediately and eternally altered.

Never let go of those moments or those miracles.

DAY 1 CHALLENGE

Are you longing to know God better? Does your heart burn when you sense the Spirit of God and hear or read the Word of God? Do you desire more of God each day, or has your love for God faded?

To refresh your feelings of love toward God, write about your journey together. Begin with the first day you truly understood His love for you. Remember the special times when He made His presence and power known just to you. If a familiar song better expresses your love for God, use those words to stir up the embers of your heart.

To ignite an inextinguishable flame in your heart for God today, watch expectantly for every moment and every miracle that is sent to overwhelm you with His love. Take note of it. Claim it as yours, and don't let anyone diminish its significance or dismiss it as coincidence.

Today God sent me a release from temptation and I took it from him gratefully.

God has renewed a friendship for me this week, one that I need desperately.

God has also brought a relationship opportunity into my life. I am very thankful.

ignited by passion

DAY 2:
A LOVE THAT LASTS

It's intriguing to watch the beginning stages of romance between two people falling in love. The signs are easy to recognize because of the sheer intensity of everything the new couple feels and does. They constantly touch each other—whether it's holding hands, kissing, or just sitting closely together. They go out of their way to see each other. They spend hours talking to each other and think nothing of picking up a phone just to check in, even if the last marathon conversation ended only an hour ago. They do whatever they can to spend as many waking hours together as possible!

Their love is all-consuming.

Their love is "on fire."

But every new couple's affection and attention is tested. Disappointment, unresponsiveness, busyness, miscommunication, and reality consumes more of their time, and the love begins fading. It becomes less important to talk, less necessary to meet, less exciting to see each other. They are no longer desperate for each other.

Romantic love and being in love with God can be very similar experiences!

You've undoubtedly known someone who was touched, healed, forgiven, or given a second chance by God, and they just can't stop thanking Him or talking to others about Him. They might unashamedly blurt out, "Praise the Lord!" when something great happens. They see, hear, and feel God in everything.

I often tell people that after God first rescued me, I became the kind of Christian that even Christians don't like being around! Have you seen those kinds of people? They can't stop talking about God. They are driven by thoughts such as, *How can I know God better? How can I serve Him?* They walk around saying things like, "You won't believe what God did today! I can't wait to see what He has in store tomorrow!"

I was effusive in my love for God. I believed every challenge I faced was merely God providing an opportunity to perform a miracle. I was certain of His love for me and my love for Him. I talked to God about *everything*—even the seemingly petty things in my life. I kid you not, I would walk into the grocery store and say, "Lord, which head of lettuce should I buy?" The spirituality of lettuce (or lack of it) isn't the point. I was simply so captivated by the Lord that I wanted Him involved in every thought, decision, and conversation.

But for most believers, there comes a time in our relationship with God when the urgency to know and be known by

God begins diminishing. Routine replaces adventure, and other priorities and passions compete for our hearts, minds, and days.

In his book *The God Who Comes*, Carlo Carretto calls it like he sees it: "If you are not searching for a personal relationship with God, if you don't stay with him for long periods in order to know him, study him, understand him, little by little you will start forgetting him, your memory will weaken, you will no longer recognize him. You will not be able to, because you will no longer know how to love."[3]

Carretto gives a great example. "If a fiancé telephones his fiancée to tell her, 'I'm sorry, this evening I can't come, I've so much work!' there is nothing wrong. But if it is the thousandth time he has made the same call, he has not been to see her in weeks on the excuse of work or outings with friends, it is more serious—rather, it is quite clear: this is not love."[4]

What is the secret of being in an ongoing, exciting, vibrant relationship with God? How can you and I love Him with all of our beings? Remember, Jesus commanded us to "love the Lord your God with *all your heart, all your soul, all your mind, and all your strength*" (Mark 12:30; emphasis added).

Maybe it's time to ask, "When will I quit making excuses for my spiritual laziness? What must I do to remove the distractions in my relationship with God? Who or what are the other 'loves' in my life? How can I remain so fully in love with God that I am a constant reflection of His presence?"

My husband, Roger, is a pastoral counselor, and he often counsels couples whose marriages are in real trouble. They tell him the love they once had is simply gone. One thing Roger asks these couples to do is talk about what it was like when they were first in love. What did they do? Where did they go? What made them feel valued by the other person?

As they go through this exercise, Roger encourages couples to recreate the dates and habits they once had. As they force themselves back into a pattern of going to special places, dressing up for each other, buying flowers, taking walks together, leaving the stress of work and kids behind, listening to one another, touching each other sweetly, and simply being in each other's presence, often the couples are reminded of why they fell in love in the first place.

In Revelation 2:4–5, God pours out His heart to His bride, the church, and says, "But I have this complaint against you. You don't love me or each other as you did at first! Look how far you have fallen!"

In the classic book *The Practice of the Presence of God*, Brother Lawrence, a seventeenth-century Carmelite priest, revealed the secrets of staying in a moment-by-moment love relationship with God. Brother Lawrence had the ability to see, hear, and feel God in the simplest chores and most mundane activities. His thoughts were captured in letters to those who struggled deeply to know and love God—in suffering and waiting or while attending to the simple routines of daily life.

Brother Lawrence suggested four practical ways to sustain a deep, unquenchable passion for God. First, *be aware and thoughtful toward God in everything you say and do*. It sounds elementary, but for some of us, being considerate of anyone other than ourselves is extremely difficult. Yet if we follow this simple instruction and give God overriding consideration in all things, how much would it change our lives? Many of us would have to acknowledge how often we take God's love for granted. We act as if we are entitled to His love, and our actions and attitudes reflect great inconsideration.

Putting this one idea into practice requires that we no longer react or respond impulsively, selfishly, angrily, or recklessly. To sincerely honor the holy God with our lives, we must consistently, instead of sporadically, confess that our disobedient, lazy, rebellious, or sinful habits *hurt* Him!

Sustaining a vibrant, deeply committed love toward God requires that we never lose sight of His love toward us, that we treat Him—by our actions and words—with the respect and honor that He deserves.

Brother Lawrence's second point was just as challenging: *be humble.* Humility is the very tangible, obvious trait of one who is controlled by, indebted to, and inspired through the living, loving God. The humble man or woman is not driven by arrogance or prominence or fame. Humility is easy to spot: when pride, arrogance, deceit, or selfishness are present, humility is not. If you desire to reflect the power, person, and presence of God . . . you must be humble.

Third, *enjoy God.* People who continuously practice the presence of God—who effortlessly think about Him, walk and talk with Him—have determined to do so for one reason: they simply enjoy being with Him. They aren't under a guilt trip to spend time with God; they are happy to do so!

Talking to God about anything and everything is a precious part of our relationship with Him—a part that most of us do not fully utilize. Okay, so maybe you wouldn't talk to God about picking a head of lettuce. Maybe you want to talk to God about a difficult co-worker or a habit you are trying to break. Sometimes you might just need to tell Him you feel lonely. Perhaps you're in your car and a song reminds you that God is faithful. Praise Him right then and there; tell Him how great He is. Practicing the presence of God should include remaining in an ongoing conversation with Him.

Finally, *let go of your fears, fall into His arms, and refuse to base your relationship with Him on feelings or circumstances.* Brother Lawrence proclaims that we love an invisible God who asks us to trust Him. Implicit to experiencing God's presence in our lives is releasing control of our lives into His care and completely depending upon Him.

Those who truly know God, above all else, believe that He is good and that He loves them. They have decided to trust Him, no matter what they're going through, no matter what they are feeling, just as Jesus trusted His Father, even as He hung on the cross.

DAY 2 CHALLENGE

Every love relationship is tested at some point. Distractions, disappointments, and discouragement can tempt your faithfulness or cause your level of trust to waver. It is no different with God. Know that times of testing *will* come in your relationship with God. A mature, not infatuated, love is required of you.

Be strengthened by the deep and underlying convictions of those whose love for God never faded. Nineteenth-century English evangelist George Muller was one who, in his sixty-plus-year relationship with God, could say, "In the greatest difficulties, in the heaviest trials, in the deepest poverty and necessities, He has never failed me; but because I was enabled by His grace to trust Him He has always appeared for my help. I delight in speaking well of His name."[5]

Today, practice the presence of God in every area of your life, in every hour of your day. In the big things—your fears and tears, your dreams and delays—draw nearer to God in your thoughts and words more than in the hour before. And in the small things—while typing a report for school, making a phone call at work, or picking up your kids from soccer practice—look for God. Ask for His presence. Talk to Him about it all, and be purposeful in delighting in God's constant company. This is how to sustain a love that will last a lifetime.

As John Wesley wrote, "Pray, just as you are led, without reasoning, in all simplicity. Be a little child, hanging on Him that loves you."[6]

Take some time to remember what it was like when God's love first met you. Recall the way you watched for Him, called on Him, set aside time to meet Him, and remained content in His presence alone.

DAY 3:
FAITH COMES
FROM HEARING

God asks every believer in every generation to live by faith, to believe without sight, and to hope with certainty and not by evidence. Hundreds of volumes of books, including every book in the Bible, record the journeys of those who believed—without ever seeing—the invisible God.

The more we read, the more evidence we uncover that faith is the only way for ordinary men and women to be in dynamic relationships with a supernatural God. By faith, we believe that God exists and has a plan for our lives. By faith, we believe that He speaks to us, confides in us, and will give us the extraordinary courage and indomitable power we need to do what He asks of us.

The eleventh chapter of Hebrews is often referred to as the "Hall of Faith," because it chronicles the history of radical, faith-filled God followers who refused to be stopped or swayed by reason or rationale. They shared the supernatural ability to believe in the impossible, to obey without a full understanding of the outcome, and to do unusual, sometimes even impractical feats to honor God's name.

For example, Noah is commended for his faith to build an ark on dry land with no rain in sight. Because of his faith, Noah built the vehicle to save mankind from an all-consuming flood! And Joshua's faith is applauded because he obeyed an order from God to march seven times around a fortress wall in the city of Jericho and blow the trumpets before bringing it down with a shout! What military leader would use musical instruments to break down a wall? Only one who absolutely trusted his unseen God to lead and save His people *could* or *would* do such things.

And Abraham is revered for holding fast to God's promise to give him a son, though he and his wife were beyond child-bearing years. After twenty-five years of waiting, and against all reasonable physical conditions, Abraham and Sarah had a son . . . just as God promised.

Where are the Abrahams, Joshuas, and Noahs of today?

Who, today, would dare believe God for the impossible and act out their faith in such outrageous ways?

I am absolutely convinced that indomitable faith is not just for the spiritually elite! Too few of us believe that what God says will actually happen. We have become a generation that lives by the motto, "I'll believe it when I see it." This is not a faith that pleases God.

Anyone can have a fired-up faith *if* it is built on . . .

> the person of God,
>> the Word of God, and
>>> the Spirit of God.

Charles Spurgeon taught that there are three stages of faith that develop with maturity: seeing, relying, and seeking. He said, "While the first level of faith believes when our emotions are favorable, the second believes when all feelings are absent. And the third level transcends the other two, for it is faith that believes God and His Word when circumstances, emotions, appearances, people, and human reason all seem to urge something to the contrary."[7]

Throughout a believer's entire life, the need to exercise faith never ceases.

God seldom shows us the way before we step out. God never breaks through before we move first. And with each test of our faith, we grow and mature as we find God trustworthy . . . not because we have first seen, but because He can be trusted. Therefore, if you do not want to toss and turn, or doubt and flail, you must rely upon something unchangeable.

Faith comes from hearing the voice of God. And reading God's Word is the most tangible way to build a faith that does not need to see in order to believe and obey. When faith is based on God's Word, it burns with inextinguishable fire for the living God. A faith that is based on Scripture is a faith that spreads, consumes, and is visible!

In *The Inner Life*, Andrew Murray writes of his own experience:

The Word gives me guidance for prayer, telling me what God will do for me. It shows me the path of prayer, telling me how God would have me come. It gives me the power for prayer, the courage to accept the assurance that I will be heard. And it brings me the answer to prayer, as it teaches what God will do for me. And so prayer prepares the heart for receiving the Word from God Himself, for the teaching of the Spirit which gives spiritual understanding, and for the faith that carries out God's will.[8]

The pattern I have used to hear God's voice for more than twenty years is to listen to Him by reading selections from the Old Testament, New Testament, Psalms, and Proverbs. I use the *Change Your Life Daily Bible,* a 365-day Bible that allows me to read through the Bible in one year.[9] It's a simple formula that never feels elementary or repetitive. God's voice is living and dynamic on each and every page of the Bible.

Through the Scripture reading on any given day, I receive advice for myself, answers for others, encouragement during waiting times, correction for my life, assurance that God is aware of my situation, and great comfort in times of trial. It never fails.

On April 27, the day my father died, the last verse of the New Testament reading for that day was Luke 23:43: "Jesus replied, 'I assure you, today you will be with me in paradise.'" I wasn't shocked. I didn't consider that verse a coincidence but a word from God to comfort my family and me. Why did I possess the faith to believe my dad was in a great place and that I would see him again? Because I heard the Lord tell me it was so.

God's Word wasn't accidental or coincidental to me on January 2, either. Roger and I were hurting from the previous day's emotional family powwow. We struggled to help our son discern God's ways, as he was a new college student who no longer lived at home and now resisted the old family rules. Our counsel was rejected by a son who wanted to live his own life. It was discouraging and even scary to us as parents.

That morning, we read from Proverbs 1:8–9: "My child, listen when your father corrects you. Don't neglect your mother's instruction. What you learn from them will crown you with grace and be a chain of honor around your neck." Admittedly, these verses were probably more comforting to us than to Jake, but I knew God was speaking words of affirmation to Roger and me as we walked through unfamiliar parental territory that didn't feel good but that we believed, in faith, was right.

God's faithfulness to speak gets me excited about reading my Bible every day. I simply don't want to miss His voice. I don't want to miss His counsel or thoughts, knowing that His Word will impact my decisions. I believe He knows how my day will unfold before it even begins, so why wouldn't I talk to Him and listen to Him? And truthfully, I am never too fired up or too strong in my faith not to need His instruction!

If you want a deep, indomitable faith, then I encourage you

to fuel it by choosing to hear God's voice and dismissing the other noises and distractions. Through the Word, God will give thoughts, directions, correction, comfort, or whatever you need for that day. Our living, loving God desires to lead us down His road of life. It may be a tough road, but it will never be the wrong road.

Be aware that when you neglect to read the Bible, you are purposely cutting yourself off from being encouraged by His voice or receiving very important and specific directions for the day, week, month, and beyond. One of the pastors at my church recently referred to "getting a download from God" whenever he hears the Lord speaking through prayer and the Word. God loves to communicate with us. He wants us to tune our hearts to Him so that in a crowded room of opinions and temptations, there is just one voice we recognize and walk toward.

Faith grows exponentially according to our time spent in the Word and prayer. Romans 10:17 (NIV) says, "Consequently, faith comes from hearing the message, and the message is heard through the word of Christ."

Instead of saying, "I *have* to spend time with God," I encourage you to say, "I don't want to miss God's voice today!"

DAY 3 CHALLENGE

If you have not made a commitment to read your Bible daily, begin today by making a decision to spend time in the Word each day for the rest of your life. As a new believer, my husband

1-7

was challenged to make this commitment more than thirty years ago. He believes this one decision has remained the most life-changing discipline of his continued spiritual growth.

Commit to a specific plan for reading the Bible. For many years I have used the *Change Your Life Daily Bible* and have found it to be a very easy way to read through the entire Bible every year. I highly recommend using a 365-day Bible, and in addition, you may want to follow a devotional or use a Bible study that walks through one book or subject at a time.

One other idea: as a young Christian, I was encouraged to listen to the Bible on tape in the same way I used to listen to music in the car or at home—often! This is a particularly helpful way for new believers, those who struggle with their thought lives, or those who are unfamiliar with God's voice to quickly know and understand God better.

DAY 4:
RESCUE PRAYING

In order to stay continually on fire for God, it is critical to know that there is an enemy who desires to see you fail, lose, and fall apart rather than be a fully devoted follower of the living God!

In 1 Peter 5:8, Peter warns fellow believers about this enemy, giving advice on how to protect ourselves against his schemes. He says, "Stay alert! Watch out for your great enemy, the devil. He prowls around like a roaring lion, looking for someone to devour."

It is essential that you know what you believe about this enemy. Is the devil all-powerful? No. Does he know our weaknesses? Yes. (Don't kid yourself: most people who know us, know our weaknesses!) Is our enemy ruthless, sneaky, and deceitful? Yes.

As an alcoholic with more than twenty-seven years of sobriety, my experience with one vice has given me great insight with other out-of-control areas of my life. Hitting bottom is something one never forgets, yet people often relapse into their previous harmful behavior. Why?

Perhaps no one wants to believe they are vulnerable. But if you are hiding or covering up your weaknesses and flaws from others, you are simply protecting your freedom to relapse. By not coming clean with others, or being accountable, you remain free to dabble in your sin or addiction without anyone knowing or stopping you. But admitting your shortcomings means you can never "slip" in front of others without intervention, support, and ultimately transformation.

One of the most freeing and yet humiliating confessions I ever made was saying, "I'm an alcoholic. I am never able to have a drink . . . ever. And I am fully aware I'll never become immune to the effects of alcohol."

Admitting you have a problem or that your life is out of control is a humbling step for anyone. Just fill in the blank with your weakness: anger, food, money, sex, lust, gambling, or procrastination, to name a few. If instead of feeding your heart for God, you feed the dangerous fire of your addiction or weakness— even a little bit—you will start a destructive blaze that can burn out of control, consuming your time, energy, affections, and appetite with nothing left for the God you claim to love.

Every one of us has one or more areas where we are vulnerable. It is critical to identify those areas and understand that we have an enemy . . .

who knows just how, where, or when to tempt us to go
back to our weakness and
whose goal it is to steal us away from God's desires and
plan for our lives.

In the book of Psalms, the writers pray often for rescue, deliverance, and salvation. They were in constant communication with God about their need for a very real experience of His power to deliver them. They did not see prayer as a last resort but as an immediate resource for deliverance from their fiercest enemy—both seen and unseen! They repeatedly cried, "Rescue me!" until they received God's power through deliverance.

As a brand-new believer in Christ, I was physically tempted, mentally barraged, and invited by friends to return to my old ways of using drugs, smoking dope, drinking alcohol, and engaging in sex outside of marriage. Hardly an hour went by when I wasn't encouraged to turn away from God.

I am so grateful that the janitor not only warned me about the unseen enemy who comes with thoughts and opportunities to steal my resolve, hope, and dreams, but he also taught me how to fight him.

Within days of becoming a Christian, I discovered a form of prayer that I call "rescue praying." Rescue praying is simply this: when you see or feel an attack coming toward you through a person who invites you to do something you resolved not to do, or as a tempting thought that pops into your mind, you must first recognize the attack for what it is—trouble and lies—and then ask Jesus to turn the thought or person away! Silently (or even out loud) say the words, "In the name of Jesus, get away from me!"

The real secret behind rescue praying is to use it not only in those moments of dire need, but *every time* you are threatened, frightened, tempted, or swayed to give in, let down your guard, speak hurtful words, wound another by your actions, or break a vow. Cultivating the habit of rescue praying in your daily life is one of the best ways I know to experience God's ever-present power to deliver. You have a choice each day, with each thought and each action. How you respond will either fuel the fire of your weaknesses or strengthen the blaze in your heart for God.

Another truth to consider is that those with burning hearts catch the attention of Satan as he searches for people to devour. Our lives are like beacons with bright spotlights! Often, the closer you come to the center of God's will, the greater your heart may burn and the stronger the attacks may become. You must understand that you are a threat to Satan. He will do anything and everything to thwart God's work in and through you. He will lie, rationalize, excuse, lure, seduce, and entice. So if you are feeling particularly tempted or challenged, be encouraged! Grasp tightly to the hand of God and claim the power of His name to rescue you always.

DAY 4 CHALLENGE

Today, identify your specific and unique weaknesses in writing.

Perhaps you are a person who struggles with anger. Until you determine that your anger is not just a bad habit but that it is sin, you will continually relapse, repeating your outbursts and tantrums. I am ashamed to say that I lived like that for years. I finally admitted to God and to others (in a letter) that my anger was keeping me from fulfilling God's plan for my life. Anger was hurting my relationships with my family and co-workers, and it was seriously diminishing the fire in my heart for God. Once I became accountable to others for "anger sobriety" and developed the habit of recognizing trouble in advance and saying a rescue prayer until I knew, felt, or saw the deliverance to overcome my struggle, I experienced real victory in this area.

Or maybe you are one of the millions of people who struggle with an addiction to food, drugs, sex, gambling, alcohol, or other destructive habits. I am convinced that your greatest asset is rescue praying! As many times as those thoughts enter your mind, images come across your television, or invitations come into your e-mail Inbox . . . you must say, "In the name of Jesus, get out of here!"

Whatever your weakness or struggle, the very next time you hear, see, or sense a roaring lion coming to steal your resolve, pray a simple but all-powerful rescue prayer!

ignited by passion

DAY 5:
STAND IN THE GAP

A burning heart can never be self-contained. It is consumed by the awesome privilege and heavy burden of reaching out to the wounded, hurting, and lost. When we are truly filled with the Holy Spirit, we cannot help but possess God's heart for people who need Him.

But often, fulfilling the call to lead people to Christ or walk with them through struggles is a long, hard, intense fight that can go on for years without visible results. Perhaps you know the pain of a prodigal child, a spouse who rejects your faith, or a friend who truly needs God but has never opened his or her heart to Him. Maybe your heart aches for a neighborhood overwhelmed by despair or for students who desperately need Jesus.

Your passion for others to know God and His love for them is a result of spending time alone with Him and letting Him share His heart with you.

E. M. Bounds was adamant about the strategic role of prayer *on behalf of others*. He said, "Talking to men for God is a great thing, but talking to God for men is greater still. He will never talk well and with real success to men for God who has not learned well how to talk to God for men."[10]

Those with burning hearts understand that talking to God for others is the place to find answers on how to reach those who are lost and seeking! As former Senate chaplain Peter Marshall was known for saying, prayer is where we get our marching orders from the Captain.

I believe that standing in the gap between God and those who reject Him—our parents, children, co-workers, neighbors, fellow students, teachers, or government leaders—is where the real battle is waged and won!

As a brand-new Christian, I returned home to my Midwestern, churchgoing family and declared that I had become a Christian. They looked at me and asked cynically, "What do you think you've been all your life?" I realized I had a lot of work to do in explaining my changed life. But the even greater mission was inviting my parents to enter into a personal relationship with God, rather than simply possessing a religious tradition.

Prayer was the place I asked God for words, verses, ideas, help, and understanding. It was through prayer that I gained the courage to live a godly life in front of my parents and to share Him every chance I had.

My changed life convinced my parents that my newfound peace, joy, and love were things they wanted for themselves.

Soon they began joining me at a church near our home, where we opened the Bible together. As a family, we began (as we had never done before) praying together. Within a few short months, both of my parents asked Christ to be the Lord of their lives.

Also in my early Christian experience, most of my peers couldn't grasp how or why I was changing so quickly—and truthfully, some didn't like the changes. I was being transformed right in front of their eyes, yet it only irritated them when I referred to God as the one who made me new! Often I prayed that they would ask me about Him, and many of them did; but most of them simply weren't ready to hear the truth.

It was a frustrating time for all of us, and soon my friends and I had very little in common. It eventually became evident that I needed to let go of many old friends in order to start a new life. But as I began to pray for new friends, I never stopped praying for my old ones. And through the years, I reconciled with most of them through e-mail, phone conversations, or get-togethers. Many of them entered into a personal relationship with God, which sparked a renewal and deepening in our friendship.

As a youth worker, I found prayer was my greatest resource! I could never fully know the life stories of every student I met, but I asked God to give me sensitivity and relevance to the kids. I especially asked God to connect me with those who were looking for love and with those who were resistant to it.

During a ten-year period, I spent hours praying for students by name. Daily, I wrote their needs and struggles in my prayer notebook, asking God to protect and guide them. I have the greatest stories of answered prayer and changed lives. In the years since, I've received numerous baby notices, wedding invitations, Christmas cards, and e-mail from former students who grew up and later located me to acknowledge my prayers and concern for them! They recognized my willingness to stand in the gap for them when they didn't even welcome the prayers. Many who grew up in homes with unbelieving parents realized that I was one of the only people who had been praying for them!

But it is as a mother that I am most willing and determined to stand in the gap. Most parents love their children before they are even born and will do anything for them. But parents who do not diligently and regularly stand in the gap—through prayer—for their children are missing out on one of the greatest calls and responsibilities in their lives.

My son, Jacob, was four years old when I began praying one hour a day. As part of my daily quiet time, I decided to have a "Jacob" page in my notebook. Every three months I started a fresh page, carrying over any unanswered prayers and listing new names of friends or teachers, new sports teams and goals, and any new classes or pending decisions.

It became a running joke in our family that whenever a new friend of Jake's walked through the door, I'd say, "Hi, what's your name?" As soon as they responded, I'd say, "Okay, thanks," and immediately write the name on Jake's page in my prayer notebook. When it seemed appropriate, I'd say, "I'm praying for you!" And they'd often give me a look as if to say, "Oh no, I wish you weren't," fearing that my prayers might keep them out of the trouble they actually enjoyed!

Through Jake's elementary school and junior high years, my prayers for him mostly related to schoolwork and friends, overcoming procrastination, and his relationship with God. But a defining moment for me came on his seventeenth birthday. I was reading from the book of Psalms that morning and opened to Psalm 135:4: "For the LORD has chosen Jacob to be his own, Israel to be his treasured possession" (NIV).

I felt as if God was talking right to me about my son, Jacob. I could almost hear Him saying, "I know today is Jake's birthday. I have a call on his life, Becky. He is my treasured possession, and I want you to more diligently, more fervently pray *and fast* for him."

I was never much of a fasting woman, but that day I determined to become one! Beginning that week and continuing through Jake's final year of college, his dad and I not only prayed daily but also set aside time each week to fast and pray for our son.

We prayed for his protection against temptation, and we continued to pray for each of his friends by name. We knew at times we were fighting battles in prayer for him, often fearing the choices he was making. We could sense there were difficult times as Jake struggled to find his own way. He made it clear that he wanted the freedom to make his own decisions, on his own terms and in his own time.

After college, Jake experienced a lull in his life and had no real direction. We continued praying and regularly fasting for our son. At that point, I discovered a book called *Praying the Scriptures for Your Children.*[11] Each chapter focused on a specific area of a child's life: career, engagement, time or money management, struggles, etc. I chose a few significant chapters and began praying the corresponding verses for Jake every day.

One year later, Jake took a job as a physical education teacher and athletic director at a small Christian school near our home. It was a very specific answer to our prayers. The job fit well with Jake's skills, gifts, and passions, but it was difficult for many other reasons. We could only surmise that God was working deeply in Jake's life, though we weren't privy to how, what, or why. We decided to step up our prayers and fasting for him. His dad and I committed to the same day, same time each week to fast and pray for Jake.

At the end of his second year as a teacher, Jake became restless. Something was shifting, but he didn't seem open to sharing his thoughts or direction with us.

At the age of twenty-five, Jake was ready for something different and decided not to teach for a third year. As the school year ended, he planned to take a month-long trip out of the country and consider his options. Again, we kept up our prayers and even asked close friends to pray for Jake, knowing he was struggling to make some big decisions in his life.

The morning Jake was supposed to leave the country, he came into the kitchen and said, "I'm not sure I should go on this trip." He was concerned about a nagging toothache, but I couldn't help but wonder if this was God's way of presenting him with other options.

If Jake stayed in the country, a family reunion, a possible job interview with a sports/mission organization in Ohio, and a retreat in Michigan could all fall into place for him in a few short weeks. Leaving the country meant missing all of that. Jake agonized over the decision, but he finally decided to forgo the overseas trip and go on the two-week trip in the States instead.

During every day of that two-week period, Jake's life changed. His heart was broken and ignited in love for the living, loving God, and most excitedly, he was infused with a passion for others to know Him. He returned home a completely different person. And the fire in his life is still brightly and wonderfully lit after many months!

I have the advantage of hindsight. I prayed for someone for more than twenty years and am able to say that I have proof that daily prayer and regular fasting results in answers, change, intervention, and fulfilled dreams.

I am convinced that if you will stand in the gap for others, you too will see God's power released, specific prayers answered, and lives touched and changed for the better.

DAY 5 CHALLENGE

Today, begin a very specific prayer request list and refer to it daily. Date the page(s) and update and/or rewrite it monthly or quarterly, depending upon how often and how many of your prayers are answered. Pray specific, rather than general, prayers for your family, neighbors, politicians, pastors, and especially yourself. Incorporate Scripture verses into your prayers. (This is a great way to learn how to pray!)

George Muller's biography records that he prayed more than sixty years for one of his friends to come to Christ. Shortly after Muller died, his friend indeed became a Christian!

Never give up praying for those whom God puts on your heart.

ignited by passion

DAY 6:
KEEP COMING

A famous Oswald Chambers quote says what so many of us feel: "Man's greatest stress is waiting on God." Those of us who have spent any amount of time waiting on God know the truth behind this statement.

Waiting can feel unbearably lonely, quiet, and unending.

Nineteenth-century English preacher Charles Spurgeon, known to preach to tens of thousands on any given Sunday, wrote, "Delayed answers to prayer are not only trials of faith; they also give us opportunities to honor God through our steadfast confidence in Him even when facing the apparent denial of our request."[12]

No one looks forward to waiting. Many of us jump at opportunities to do something adventurous, or even daring. But no one expects to move in an exciting direction, seemingly at God's command, only to be disappointed or rejected or stalled or ridiculed. Yet Noah, Abraham, Moses, Joseph, Elijah, and even Jesus stepped out, following God's call . . . and then experienced delay, discouragement, and days—even years—in a desert, jail, pit, or wilderness.

We learn from their lives that the desert, the waiting place, is not a place of punishment. It is a place of preparation, testing, and developing a trust in God. It is a time for listening *only* to God's voice so that when many other voices are present, we can recognize *only* God's voice, as we discussed a few days ago. It is a time of holding on to the invisible, the impossible, even the irrational and watching and waiting for God to bring rescue.

When God asked His servants to step aside, wait, or be still—they obeyed. They accomplished God's purpose, in His time and in His way. And so very often, their obedience to wait on God resulted in an unbelievably significant manifestation of His power to change the course of a family or even a nation.

In my deepest, darkest disappointments, which have seemingly come more often in the past few years, I can honestly say that I do not feel like giving up. I must tell you, I feel very strongly that I *must not* give up! I don't hear many voices telling me to "keep coming," but I do hear *God* whisper and sometimes even shout those very words to me.

When I wake up day after day and wonder . . .

Why so long, Lord? or

How much longer?

I may not get an answer that day that changes my circumstances, but I am always consoled and comforted by God's Word. I am truly encouraged, knowing that David, in the Psalms, cried out the very same words. I am fueled with hope when I know that God called many to stand firm, wait long, and hope against hope.

I'm convinced that those who . . .

give up on their call,

let go of the dream God has put in their heart,

falter, waver, and even fall hard

have, early on, when they are discouraged or disappointed with their circumstances, quit spending time with God.

They quit listening to the only voice that really counts. Their fire fades and they abandon their call because they've cut off their source of supernatural power! They've gone into the desert and died of thirst, rather than refueling their minds and hearts with unending encouragement from God Himself. They no longer follow His directions; instead, they assume or presume or respond impulsively or fearfully. And without God's fire, they lack the physical, mental, and emotional strength it takes to persevere.

If you are called to do *anything* great or small for God, you will have to persevere—when you don't feel like it, when it doesn't seem fair, and when you're tired. First Peter 1:6—7 speaks a defining word of encouragement to all believers who sense great battle, struggle, or delay:

So be truly glad. There is wonderful joy ahead, even though you have to endure many trials for a little while. These trials will show that your faith is genuine. It is being tested as fire tests and purifies gold—though your faith is far more precious than mere gold. So when your faith remains strong through many trials, it will bring you much praise and glory and honor on the day when Jesus Christ is revealed to the whole world.

If and when you . . .
    are sidelined;
If and when you . . .
    feel abandoned, imprisoned, or rejected;
If and when you . . .
    seem silenced and misunderstood;
If and when you . . .
    are thirsty in a desert or wandering in a wilderness,
you are most vulnerable to letting your burning heart for God be snuffed out and extinguished.

Against all odds, against the tide, against the pressure, against the lies of Satan or even the voices of friends who can no longer bear to see you suffer, you must not let your fire fade, dim, or go out. Do not abandon your call. Whatever God has asked of you or required of you, don't run from it. Don't quit because it is too hard. You must neither let your passion die nor your heart give up.

DAY 6 CHALLENGE

Oh, my fellow Burning Heart sojourner, if you've made it this far, you've just got to "keep coming." One hour, one day at a time, put yourself in the presence of God. Open His Word and surround yourself with teachers and authors who speak and write biblical truth and breathe Holy Spirit-filled fire into your life.

DAY 7:
HOUR OF POWER

On the day I spoke for chapel at Azusa Pacific University in the fall of 2004, I came off the platform and immediately told the chaplain I needed to come back—not next year or next semester, but the next week. The Holy Spirit did an amazing work, inspiring hundreds of kids to get excited about prayer. The commitment to spend one hour a day with God was passionate and overwhelming. But I knew I had to return the following week and show them how to pray—how to fill that hour with power!

When I returned to the campus the next week, I told the students that I was back because I didn't want them to fail. We all sensed the Holy Spirit's presence calling us to a lifetime of rich conversation with God, but there was no way in the previous week's short chapel service that I could adequately equip them with the tools they needed to launch out on their great adventure. So, in the second talk, I shared the specific how-to ideas that have guided and sustained me for two decades.

I trust you are also feeling a great passion to spend more time with God by now. And just like the students who were called and inspired to know God more fully, I want you to truly succeed and discover the abundance waiting for you through daily conversations with God.

I started with the students by explaining that when I decided to pray, the amount of time I chose—one hour—was very matter-of-fact. Perhaps I was unafraid to make such a big commitment because as a wife, mom, and youth worker, I had numerous, important one-hour appointments on my calendar every day. Workouts, television shows, staff meetings, club meetings, luncheons, and telephone calls filled my schedule. Yet the glaring void on my calendar was that I never made time for God.

At that convention in February 1984, I decided to spend one hour a day with God for the rest of my life because I knew that if I could easily spend one-hour increments on any given day doing everything else I wanted to do, I could certainly have a daily appointment with God!

In the weeks after, back home in my kitchen each morning, I sat down with a notebook, pen, Bible, and a cup of coffee. I even set the alarm to get up one hour earlier than ever before. And I freely, enthusiastically, and expectantly talked to God and listened to Him.

It was exhilarating to write down my thoughts, feelings, hopes, dreams, and specific requests. It was humbling to write out my confessions. But it was simply awesome to hear God respond! Sometimes His answers came very quickly; other times I waited for days or months for God to answer me.

And because God answered so many of my prayers, I loved sharing my experience with my family, club kids, and staff members. Soon everyone began asking me to teach them how to write their prayers.

I wanted to know more about prayer! One of my favorite authors, Leonard Ravenhill, wrote extensively on the power of prayer. In his book *Revival Praying*, I found incredible nuggets such as, "No man is greater than his prayer life" and "The people who pray most, accomplish most"![3]

But it was Andrew Murray who really opened my eyes with his famous quote: "The devil's greatest tool is to keep the believer from praying."

At that time, I asked God for a design for prayer that I could share with others. If we are to commit to praying daily, we must have a plan for making the most of our time with Him. I talk to many people who tell me they simply don't know how to pray. They tell me they run out of things to pray about within the first ten minutes.

So, during one of those early hours of prayer, I wrote down a very specific plan that I have used for more than twenty years and have shared with thousands. The pieces came together in a journal I developed called *My Partner Prayer Notebook*. As I mentioned previously, this journal has two parts: "God's Part" and "My Part."

In "My Part," I write four types of prayers, using the acronym PART:

Praise—I begin by telling God how great He is! I use the Psalms as my guide, reading 1 through 150 in consecutive order, paraphrasing every verse that shares my same feeling or thought for the day. At the same time, the psalms I am reading usually include verses that speak right back to me with real comfort or encouragement. I write these verses in my notebook as well, beginning my two-way conversations with God.

Admit—This is the section where I confess my sins in writing. I know that sounds daunting, but every day for more than twenty years, I have started by writing Psalm 139:23–24: "Search me, O God, and know my heart; test me and know my anxious thoughts. See if there is any offensive way in me . . ." (NIV), and I am always prompted to agree with God about the areas of my life in which I am struggling or falling short. I leave this section encouraged by writing out Romans 12:2, asking God to renew my mind by His powerful Holy Spirit: "Let God transform you into a new person by changing the way you think. Then you will learn to know God's will for you, which is good and pleasing and perfect."

Request—A full prayer request list has taught me that asking God, as Charles Spurgeon says, "is the rule of the kingdom, whether we like it or not!" God doesn't always answer in my time or in the way I want . . . but God answers prayer. I follow David's example in Psalm 5:3: "In the morning, O LORD . . . I lay my requests before you and wait in expectation" (NIV).

Thanks—I finish "My Part" in prayer with a handwritten thank-you note to God, acknowledging His intervention, activity, responses, comfort, and appearance in my daily life.

In "God's Part," there are six sections: L, M, N, O, P, and To Do!

Listening—In this section, I write down the thoughts and verses and impressions that are on my heart and mind during my hour with God. But listening to God takes practice! My husband suggests that if you are not familiar or comfortable with hearing God's voice, simply write out, "Dear _____ (insert your name), I love you! Signed, God." He suggests you take a few minutes and write out what you imagine God might be saying to you. There are numerous books to help you grow in this area of your prayer life, including Jerry Bridges's book *The Pursuit of Holiness*, in which he explains that anyone can hear God's voice in four ways:

1. memorizing key passages for immediate recall,

2. hearing scriptures used in sermons,

3. studying Scripture intently for special counsel, and

4. reading the Bible regularly to know God's viewpoint in all aspects of life.[14]

Messages—This section of *My Partner Prayer Notebook* is reserved for sermon and Bible study notes. I expect God to speak to me, and I never want to miss or forget a great truth tucked within a message or testimony, so I simply take my note-book with me whenever I am going to hear a message!

New Testament,

Old Testament, and

Proverbs—In these three sections, I record the verses in my daily, planned Bible reading that touch my heart and give me impressions or direction or correction. I use the *Change Your Life Daily Bible,* a special edition of *The One Year Bible,* and I daily hear God's voice speak to me.

To Do—During my one hour with God, I get ideas and reminders to do, go, send, drop off, fulfill a commitment, make a call or send a fax, letter, or e-mail. Rather than do any or all of those things in that moment, I write them down on my To Do list in the back of *My Partner Prayer Notebook* . . . and complete the task later that day. Besides keeping me from becoming distracted, I'm amazed how much time management and organization will occur during one hour spent with God!

Why has my heart burned strongly for the living, loving God for more than two decades, even and especially during difficult times in my life? I believe it is the result of my commitment to prayer.

For every part of me that doesn't want to . . .

get up early to pray, or

put my hope out on the line one more time, or

do the right thing, or

press on when it looks hopeless,

I believe my non-negotiable commitment to spend one hour a day with God has kept my heart passionately burning with love for Him.

In my "hour of power," I am fueled to overcome any discouragement. I am given discernment to discount any voices that attempt to veer me off course. In each moment with the Lord, I am reminded of both my desire and my commitment to fulfill His call in my life.

Because I am committed to spending one hour a day with God, no matter how I feel, no matter what is going on in my life, no matter what . . . I allow His Word to daily expose any lurking lies and negative thinking.

The discipline of my time allows His Word to discipline my mind and my body.

DAY 7 CHALLENGE

It is amazing how much time we devote to things that matter to us. Whether it's outings with friends or appointments with business associates, our priorities are directly reflected in how we spend our time.

Today, look up verses in the concordance of your Bible that include the words *ask, believe,* and *pray.* Read these verses with an openness and expectation to understand how much and how often God wants you to come to Him in prayer.

As you freshly discover and acknowledge the power available

in prayer, I encourage you to make prayer a priority in your life. If you have never done so, set aside a specific amount of time on your calendar for the next two days to have an appointment with God. Pick a quiet place to meet, and have a plan for your time. Consider writing your prayers. And be sure that your time with God includes both talking to Him and listening to Him.

I am absolutely convinced that if you discover prayer, decide to pray, and have a design for prayer, your prayers will be powerful and effective!

PURIFIED BY FIRE

A. T. Pierson wrote, "Our Father, who seeks to perfect His saints in holiness, knows the value of the refiner's fire. It is with the most precious metals that a metallurgist will take the greatest care. He subjects the metal to a hot fire, for only the refiner's fire will melt the metal, release the dross and allow the remaining, pure metal to take a new and perfect shape in the mold."[15]

The procedure required to turn an impure heart into a burning heart for God is similar—only a continual refining fire will purify our motives and cleanse our character, making us beautiful and valuable treasures, useful for God's purposes. That fire is available to us in the person and presence of Christ and through the constant indwelling of the Holy Spirit.

In the 1947 signed pledge by the Fellowship of the Burning Heart, God impressed Bill Bright and his friends to define their wholehearted devotion to Him by making lifetime commitments to sobriety and sexual purity. It's worth at least considering why those two specific tenets were so important to them.

I don't believe the Fellowship of the Burning Heart forged their pledge out of legalism, but out of a desire to lead lives that burned brightly for the living, loving God. Neither do I believe they were attempting to turn people toward their way of thinking. They were, *for themselves*, deciding how best to express and maintain their passion for God, their willingness to be holy as He is, and to be powerful tools in His hand for His work and His name for a lifetime. And they invited others of like mind and conviction to join in.

The extent to which culture and society in the twenty-first century is exploiting sex, drugs, alcohol, pornography, and vulgarity, even in the Christian community, was utterly unimaginable in 1947. The fact that these followers of God saw sexual purity and sobriety as two core issues that provided maximum opportunity for either depleting or amplifying their effectiveness for God makes the tenets of their contract all the more relevant to us today.

Why is the call to holiness missing in the Christian culture of this generation? Perhaps because the call to holiness is . . .

difficult to hear,
difficult to live, and
difficult to give.

I have felt the call upon my life both to live and to give this message. My heart is guided by Paul's words in Titus 2:12–15:

We are instructed to turn from godless living and sinful pleasures. We should live in this evil world with wisdom, righteousness, and devotion to God, while we look forward with hope to that wonderful day when the glory of our great God and Savior, Jesus Christ, will be revealed. He gave his life to free us from every kind of sin, to cleanse us, and to make us his very own people, totally committed to doing good deeds. You must teach these things and encourage the believers to do them. You have the authority to correct them when necessary, so don't let anyone disregard what you say.

If there is nothing different about how we live, think, believe, and speak compared to the world around us, what evidence is there that we are truly on fire for God? If we desire to remain forever in love with and useful to God, I believe we must be convinced that God asks us to be holy—not through our own will power but through the power of His Holy Spirit within us. We must also believe that the purer and holier we are, the more powerful our impact and enthusiasm will be for the God we serve. And finally, we must acknowledge that purity and holiness mean being set apart from and different than the rest of society—something that isn't always easy or comfortable for us.

When we are convinced that those who reflect a holy God shine brightest in a dark world, we will no longer allow the absence of holiness and the presence of darkness in our lives to diminish His Spirit in us.

Paul's letters to the Corinthians, Colossians, Thessalonians, Timothy, and Titus, along with the two letters of Peter, give every generation a clear and absolute call to holy living. They repeatedly challenge and urge believers to take their salvation seriously by living lives set apart for God. I encourage you to read these New Testament letters and ask the Holy Spirit to

8-14

give you a burning heart for God through purity!

During the next seven days, let us experience a revival of God's Spirit in our hearts to set us apart.

purified by fire

DAY 8:
SIGNED, SEALED,
DELIVERED—I'M YOURS

Oswald Chambers emphasized that "when we ask God for the Holy Spirit, we receive the very nature of God, the *Holy* Spirit."[16]

My prayer in the church basement included an invitation to the Holy Spirit to fill me up to overflowing. I didn't fully understand the impact those words would immediately have upon my life. I was just so overwhelmed with the sensation of being forgiven and changed that I only wanted more of the same. My heart literally felt like it was on fire! And though I didn't understand it at the time, God's love toward me elicited a response that was nothing less than an absolute and increasing desire to be pure and holy.

From the moment I received Christ, I *felt* renewed, swept clean, and abundantly filled by something real.

It was God's Holy Spirit!

Ephesians 1:13–14 describes what I experienced: "Now you Gentiles have also heard the truth, the Good News that God saves you. And when you believed in Christ, he identified you as his own by giving you the Holy Spirit, whom he promised long ago. The Spirit is God's guarantee that he will give us the inheritance he promised and that he has purchased us to be his own people. He did this so we would praise and glorify him."

The janitor, in very simple words, explained that the Holy Spirit had sealed me, which meant I was set apart, different, changed, and destined for eternity with Christ. With complete confidence, the janitor told me that God's Holy Spirit had delivered me from a broken, empty life so that I might live a life filled with passion and purpose. Because he believed it so emphatically, he gave me courage to believe it as well. I had been desperate and despicable for so long, this was indeed good news!

I noticed immediate proof of the existence of the Holy Spirit and His seal upon my life. I saw it, and so could others around me.

I was delivered from the crushing need for others' approval.

I no longer had a desire to drink.

I was freed from depression, anxiety, addiction, and feelings of worthlessness.

I was enthusiastic and positive about God—traits that only hours and days before were completely absent.

I had *no other explanation* for the instant morality, incredible peace, and newfound sobriety I exhibited, except that God forgave me, lived in me, and filled me up to overflowing with His Holy Spirit.

Wesley Duewel was a missionary to India and the former president of OMS International, a global mission organization. He remains a revered teacher on the Holy Spirit. In his book *Ablaze for God*, Duewel writes, "The Holy Spirit is a holy *Person*, not a holy emotion. Yet as this holy Person works within us, He imparts His holy power, His divine adequacy to us in such a way that we feel new inner strength, new enablement above our own resources, a sense of special spiritual authority and faith, and we recognize a new effectiveness which we must credit entirely to the Spirit, not to ourselves."[17]

Signed, sealed, and needing incredible deliverance, I cried out to God for more of His Holy Spirit—all of His Holy Spirit. I was not shy in asking for more power and more courage and more purity. I had such great obstacles to overcome, such enormously unhealthy and ungodly habits to shake off, that if my deliverance could come simply by asking, I would ask without hesitation or reservation. Encouraged by my mentor, I made it a daily habit to ask for all the power, fruit, and gifts of the Holy Spirit that God could possibly give me.

I asked and asked and asked for more. And I was filled and filled and filled. I experienced a power that was not my own. I stood, I turned, and I overcame. I *expected* the Holy Spirit to give me power to do and say the extraordinary and the unexpected. And He did!

I look back now and realize how important it was for me to understand that I was free and delivered of my old sins. My problems were too numerous, too burdensome, too consuming, too defeating. I do not believe that I could have successfully taken a single step into my new life unless I *accepted my deliverance as fact*.

My once apathetic, broken, and defiled heart was being cleansed, ignited, and set apart for the living, loving God.

Wesley Duewel further explained the phenomenal supernatural power of the Holy Spirit upon a person's life. He said, "God has created our spirits flammable. We are spiritually combustible. Our nature is created to be set ablaze by the Spirit. We are spiritually most blessed, most victorious, most usable when we are ablaze. We are most Godlike when we glow with holy flame—the flame of the indwelling Spirit."[18]

Passion for God is ignited by His love. His presence in our lives becomes evident to all when we are signed, sealed, and delivered by the Holy Spirit of the living God, leaving His holy imprint.

I meet Christians all the time whose lives are anything but *delivered*. They might grasp the signed and sealed parts of the Holy Spirit, but they struggle to believe that God's power is present and available—right now—to help them overcome the issues choking them. Struggles such as smoking, alcohol abuse, anger, overspending, gossip, dishonesty, and sexual immorality might seem like the big issues, but for many of us, the things that enslave us are much more subtle. We make excuses for dragging around decades of guilt or feelings of unworthiness, resentment, unforgiveness, jealousy, or manipulative behavior.

Imagine for a moment what it would feel like to experience deliverance in the area in which you struggle the most. Can you sense the space in your chest expanding again? Can you feel the heaviness on your shoulders lighten? How does your outlook on life change? Does your desire to live passionately start to warm again?

My friend, you must not stop short of asking for and accepting the promised deliverance and extra measure of power that is available to you through the Holy Spirit.

The same power from on high that came upon Elijah, Nehemiah, Ezra, Mary, and David came to sign, seal, and deliver me. And it is available to you. The same hand that graciously stretched out in favor upon their lives and that came upon me is available to you. The same deliverance that rescued them and came to deliver me is available to deliver you. The same Holy Person who indwelled them physically and entered me will do the same for you. The same source of strength that altered their personalities and transformed me can change your life. The same unexplainable hope that filled their hearts and minds and came to fill me wants to fill you too.

In 2 Corinthians 1:9–10, Paul describes the refuge and faithfulness of God, even in the worst circumstances. Paul writes, "Indeed, in our hearts we felt the sentence of death. But this happened that we might not rely on ourselves but on God, who raises the dead. He has delivered us from such a deadly peril, and he will deliver us. On him we have set our hope that he will continue to deliver us" (NIV).

Notice that Paul says God *delivered* them (past tense) and *will deliver* them (future tense). This is the message! Whatever issue or struggle is holding you back; the Lord is your deliverer! Grab on to the life-changing truth that the Holy Spirit is all-powerful to purify you through His fire and make you holy today. Invite Him to set you free right now. Do not delay. Ask. And do not be afraid to keep asking.

DAY 8 CHALLENGE

How would your life change if you lived like you believed what the Bible said about being delivered from sin and being under the control of the Holy Spirit? Read the following verses, then make them your personal prayers. Rewrite them using your name and identifying your struggles. Confess that the freedoms and powers over sin are yours! Ask the Holy Spirit to take control of any area of your life that needs deliverance.

> When you were slaves to sin, you were free from the obligation to do right. And what was the result? You are now ashamed of the things you used to do, things that end in eternal doom. But now you are free from the power of sin and have become slaves of God. Now you do those things that lead to holiness and result in eternal life. For the wages of sin is death, but the free gift of God is eternal life through Christ Jesus our Lord. (Romans 6:20–23)

Those who are dominated by the sinful nature think about sinful things, but those who are controlled by the Holy Spirit think about things that please the Spirit. So letting your sinful nature control your mind leads to death. But letting the Spirit control your mind leads to life and peace. For the sinful nature is always hostile to God. It never did obey God's laws, and it never will. That's why those who are still under the control of their sinful nature can never please God. (Romans 8:5–8)

8-14

purified by fire

DAY 9:
CONSTANT COMPANION

In his book *The Holy Spirit*, Billy Graham writes, "The members of the early Church, those men, women, and children who knew the reality of the Holy Spirit, as a force, were totally transformed . . . and the glory of it for us is that He is present in every true believer today and so His power is available today."[19]

I believe many Christians are missing out on the constant source of companionship and power available to them through the presence of the Holy Spirit. People often walk away from their first encounters with God and never again ask the Holy Spirit to meet, sustain, strengthen, and deliver them. The result is a critical breakdown in their ability to sustain a burning heart for God.

If we are not constantly—and yes, I mean constantly—accessing God's Spirit of Holiness, we leave ourselves wide open to attacks, relapse, sin, impurity, and distraction from the purpose to which we are called.

When I look back on my life, I realize the church janitor possessed an unusual sense of spiritual insight and responsibility toward me. He knew that my overwhelming physical addictions and emotional problems needed more than a short-term, hope-filled message to stave off a mental, moral, or physical collapse.

Before I left the church, he was adamant that I take with me something—or *Someone*—more. Knowledgeable of the power that links God's Word and Spirit, he instructed me on how to access the supernatural, moment-by-moment counsel, discernment, and strength of God at all times.

To totally transform my current life and to *sustain* a dramatic turnaround, I needed constant spiritual companionship. The church janitor realized that the extent to which I needed transformation, no person or organization could provide. Only the Holy Spirit of the living God could ensure that my death-to-life transaction resulted in permanent transformation.

Without religious training or instruction, I seemed genuinely able to visualize the person of God in the form of His Holy Spirit breathing new power into me. The experience was more than wistful; I literally received a series of thoughts, impressions, attitudes, words, and emotions that were far above and beyond my normal standards and habits. New actions quickly followed.

But just as the janitor predicted, within hours of leaving the building, it was as if darts of doubt were assigned to assail me. The tantalizing temptations of my past, as well as the disapproval of onlookers, worked to create every possible distraction and reason to return to the old life.

How does an alcoholic build days, weeks, months, and years of sobriety?

How does a woman living with her boyfriend walk away from the man she loves and choose to live in purity?

How does a person accustomed to satisfying every lust, desire, and selfish yearning develop self-control, patience, and discipline?

Keeping my heart ablaze in the face of enormous obstacles and temptations required an intentional, constant focus on the living God while tapping into the always-open line of communication with His Holy Spirit.

John 14:16–17 says, "I will ask the Father, and he will give you another counselor to be with you forever—the Spirit of truth. The world cannot accept him, because it neither sees him nor knows him. But you know him, for he lives with you and will be in you" (NIV).

Wesley Duewel writes, "To be filled means that the whole personality is so imbued by the Spirit, pervaded by the Spirit, and saturated with the Spirit that the person is not only spiritual but Spirit-full. For you to be Spirit-filled implies that the presence and power of the Spirit rests upon your person, clothes you, and is manifest through you. It makes a decided difference in you, a new God-given dimension and a new transforming fullness in your life and leadership. You recognize it and others recognize it." [20]

Since the day I became a Christian, I have experienced tremendous transformation that is both an unexplainable mystery and a memorable miracle!

In his book *The Holy Spirit*, Billy Graham writes, "I am convinced that to be filled with the Spirit is not an option, but a necessity. It is indispensable for the abundant life and for fruitful service. . . . It is intended for all, needed by all, and available to all. This is why the Scripture commands all of us, 'Be filled with the Spirit.'"[21]

Because of my dramatic encounter with God and the immediate help I received from His Holy Spirit, I am absolutely convinced that anyone can and everyone should experience this fullness of God. The Holy Spirit is continuously available to transform anyone . . . not just today or for the next year, but for a lifetime.

Whatever challenge, dream, call, change, commitment, temptation, or fear you face, you need God's Holy Spirit to constantly guard your heart, mind, words, and life.

"Since we are living by the Spirit, let us follow the Spirit's leading in every part of our lives" (Galatians 5:25).

DAY 9 CHALLENGE

J. I. Packer, author of *Knowing God*, wrote, "Christians have an indwelling Instructor, the Holy Spirit."[22] Psalm 46:1 says, "God is our help and strength, an ever-present help in trouble" (NIV).

If you've ever participated in a Twelve-Step group, you

know the power of accountability. A newly sober person is strongly encouraged to get a "sponsor," someone whom they can call day and night when they are afraid, need to talk, or are tempted to go back to their previous lifestyle.

In an even more profound and complete way, the Holy Spirit is your constant companion, instructor, counselor, and sponsor. Whatever your struggle, no matter the time of day or the depth of your concern, He is always available to counsel and comfort you.

What is the Holy Spirit saying to you today?

8-14

DAY 10:
RESOLVE TO CHANGE

At the beginning of the twenty-first century, a new television format erupted in America. "Reality TV" became the rage, and programmers fed viewers' insatiable passion for makeover madness. Casting calls attracted people who lined up around the block to experience radical, life-changing transformation made instantaneously available to a fortunate few.

I wanted to shout to all the change seekers, "You don't have to look any further than right where you are. If you want to change your life, it is possible, obtainable, right now, today! Just run toward the powerful, transforming God of the Bible with the same passion and purpose you seek outer transformation, and God has an even better transformation for you."

I'll never forget how the janitor gave me hope by quoting 2 Corinthians 5:17: "This means that anyone who belongs to Christ has become a new person. The old life is gone; a new life has begun!"

If I had any doubt that the prayer I'd just prayed had

changed my life, these words, spoken with authority, drove those remaining doubtful thoughts away. I was different, no longer controlled by sin. I was brand-new; not just cleaned up to look and feel better, but I received a new heart, a new mind, and new eyes. I took the promise of Scripture literally. I believe these words dramatically affected the way I perceived my simple encounter with God, and they set a precedent for future changes in my life. I was given the secret to a spiritual makeover.

The apostle Paul defines a spiritual makeover as more than outward change. He identifies a transformed person as one who is dead to self and who no longer lives! He says, "My old self has been crucified with Christ. It is no longer I who live, but Christ lives in me. So I live in this earthly body by trusting in the Son of God, who loved me and gave himself for me" (Galatians 2:20).

The deep, lasting change that we all seek can happen in an instant, but it doesn't happen without an exchange. It is a transaction in which you relinquish your present life to the living, loving God and, *in return*, you receive a new way of thinking, new courage, new appetite, and even repulsion toward something you previously held on to.

It sounds incredible. And frankly, it is! So why do throngs of people jump at the chance for an outer makeover but lack any interest in achieving spiritual transformation? Are they fearful of the unknown or too addicted to temporary highs and quick fixes to enter into a long-term experience with God? Are they unaware of the incredible benefits in receiving a new life in Christ?

There is a reason.

Some people want the new life but aren't willing to give up the old one. A new life that lasts for eternity is only found in death . . . to self.

In this decision of surrender, the "worst of the worst" and the "best of the best" people share a common need: a humble desire to exchange their old lives—*just as they are*—for new, holy, and righteous lives in Christ! It is through humble surrender that the incredible power, passion, and purpose that was previously unavailable is newly released into our lives.

8-14

Sometimes the outer change that occurs is equally dramatic as the inner changes. When men and women are given . . .

> new hearts to love,
>> new eyes to see,
>>> new words to speak, and
>>>> new purpose for living,

there is a new passion for life.

This new life is not just available and relevant to those with desperate, seemingly worthless lives. God gives no favor or exemptions to the rich or poor, to the strong or weak. No labels of race or gender can lift or lower us. No prominent or insignificant titles can puff or deflate us. Education, or lack of it, will not define us.

A heart that burns with the very passions and purpose of the living, loving God requires that all men and women humbly let go of their will and surrender all of themselves to God. They must be willing to die to self. They must relinquish their old lives and exchange them for a new life in Christ.

Maybe you did this long ago but realize that somewhere along the way, you slowly started taking pieces of your old life or old nature back from God, and now you have your hands full trying to manage your chaotic or unhealthy life. Perhaps you thought He wouldn't notice if you picked up that one favorite habit again or indulged in a couple of self-centered thoughts here and there. Maybe the attraction of the world or the pain of not getting what you wanted has contributed to a loss of passion, purity, and purpose.

When you think about the fact that God requires you to submit your entire self to Him, if there is even one thing that causes you to say, "Lord, anything but that!" then this is likely the area in which God is asking you to let go, to die. Those with burning hearts must be willing to commit every area of life to God.

This is the time to seriously evaluate your life. It is the time to pray Psalm 139:23–24, which says, "Search me, O God, and know my heart; test me and know my anxious thoughts. See if there is any offensive way in me, and lead me in the way everlasting" (NIV).

DAY 10 CHALLENGE

In a powerful selection from *One Christian's Secret to a Happy Life*, Hannah Whitall Smith gives a template for experiencing release from the power of sin over your life—in essence, an instant makeover—through surrender to God.

Hannah's "sin of choice" was doubt. In the following excerpt, replace the word doubt with the specific and individual temptation that you keep taking back or tripping over. In the world of recovery, we call those takebacks, or relapses. To end your repeated relapses, there must come a day and time when, with complete resolve, you surrender this area to God.

After reading this excerpt, consider the area or areas in your life that need a fresh touch of the Holy Spirit's power and follow Hannah's lead: resolve to change!

8-14

> Like any other sin, the stronghold is in the will and the will or purpose to doubt must be surrendered exactly as you surrender the will or purpose to yield to any other temptation. God always takes possession of a surrendered will.
>
> In this matter of doubting the trouble is that the Christian does not always make a full surrender. "I do not want to doubt any more," we will say, or, "I hope I will not." But it is hard to come to the point of saying, "I will not doubt again," and no surrender is effective until one says, "I will not."
>
> Remember: we cannot give up doubting gradually. We must give it up all at once and must completely rely on the Lord for deliverance when we are tempted. The moment the assault comes, we must lift up the shield

of faith against it. We must hand the very first sugges-
tion of doubt over to the Lord, and must let Him manage it. We must refuse to entertain the doubt a single
moment. We must simply say, "I dare not doubt. I must
trust. God is my Father, and He does love me. Jesus
saves me. He saves me now." Those three little words,
repeated over and over, "Jesus saves me, Jesus saves
me," will put to flight the greatest army of doubts that
ever assaulted any soul. I have tried it many times and
have never known it to fail.[23]

purified by fire

DAY 11:
SPIRITUAL BREATHING

Breathing is the most natural and essential thing we humans do. Inhaling and exhaling is as important as food or water. In fact, we take an average of twelve to fourteen breaths each minute. We do it when we work, drive, eat, and play. It's so essential that we keep breathing even when we sleep!

In the course of Dr. Bill Bright's expansive ministry, he taught the concept of "spiritual breathing" as a way to conceptualize the act of staying filled and anointed with God's Holy Spirit. He believed that being connected to God's thoughts and presence was as elementary as breathing. To be effective, power-filled Christians, we must inhale the Spirit of God, just as we breathe oxygen into our lungs.

Bright's biography, *Amazing Faith*, recounts the profound impact spiritual breathing had on his life. He said that spiritual breathing "has enriched my life as has no other truth." That is a very weighted statement for a man who mentored tens of thousands and wrote numerous books and pamphlets used to teach hundreds of millions of seekers how to know and walk with God.

He described spiritual breathing as a "process of exhaling the impure and inhaling the pure, an exercise in faith that enables you to experience God's love and forgiveness and to walk in the Spirit as a way of life."[24]

Bright, like all believers, faced doubt, unbelief, and the personal temptations that seek to destroy each of us. He compassionately and empathetically counseled strugglers to live a Spirit-filled life with practical help. He wrote, "The failures of the flesh need not govern us. We're to deal with them promptly. Once our conscience makes us aware of a sin, we're to confront and confess it and immediately ask God to resume control, to take the driver's seat. And we're to *believe* all this will happen, because God hears the prayer of earnest people asking Him to deliver on His promises."[25]

Before your heart can burn with indomitable, relentless passion and fire for God, you must embrace the truth that the oxygen for spiritual living is dependent upon God's Holy Spirit. Therefore, your invitation to Him cannot be casual. It must be purposeful and continual, until one day it becomes as constant and as natural as breathing.

Different than time set aside in prayer, spiritual breathing willingly invites the Holy Spirit into your moment-by-moment thought life. Because so many of our thoughts are distractive, disruptive, or destructive, spiritual breathing is the habit of ridding your mind of tempting, negative thoughts and replacing—

even refueling—them with thoughts the Holy Spirit gives you.

To overcome recurring doubt, your thoughts must be constantly renewed and impressed by God's thoughts.

To fight off fear or combat negative thoughts that seek to destroy your faith, you must be continually encouraged by the Word of God.

If you embrace this idea, I believe you will rapidly close the gap in your life between the spiritual and the natural, the extraordinary and the ordinary, the impossible and the possible.

God's Spirit is powerful, efficient, and able; our spirits are weak, unfocused, and unwilling. I know by experience that one's willingness to partake in spiritual breathing will dictate one's progress in purpose-filled living.

If you desire to have passion and purpose in your life, you must allow oxygen to keep fanning the flame of God within you. Staying on fire for God takes more than intention; it requires action.

Charles Spurgeon spoke much about tending to the flame within us daily. He said, "Be consumed with love for Christ, and let the flame burn continuously, not flaming up at public meetings and dying out in the routine work of every day. We need indomitable perseverance, dogged resolution, and a combination of sacred obstinacy, self-denial, holy gentleness, and invincible courage."[26]

It is not by chance or coincidence that those who are passionate for God are breathing in the Spirit of God. They are empowered by God. Their thinking is influenced by the Holy Spirit! They see outside the box, beyond the present, and above the limits. They are not always dependent upon others to advise or rescue them. They have received God's marching orders; they are in constant communication with Him. Their prayers are not hopes and wishes but two-way conversations with the living, loving God. They constantly look to one Source for wisdom and direction. They know when to sit still and when to move. They are listening, not to their troubled thoughts, but to God's thoughts, His direction. And they recognize His voice, whether He whispers or shouts.

Most importantly, they are resolved to follow God's plan, whether it appears foolish, unusual, or uncertain. They have mastered the act of breathing in the breath of God's Spirit for courage, hope, and peace.

In *Freedom of Simplicity*, Richard Foster writes, "We must order our lives in particular ways. We must take up a consciously chosen course of action that will draw us more deeply into perpetual communion with the Father. This desire to practice the presence of God is the secret of all the saints."[27]

A secret of the burning heart lies in desire. Do you long to know God better? Are you desperate to have constant companionship with Him? Are you willing to turn your thoughts over to Him, to do whatever it takes to become power-filled and anointed?

Then take your passion and desire and turn this thirst into a daily discipline. Consciously, until it becomes unconscious . . .

- *Exhale* destructive, critical, sinful thoughts. *Inhale* positive, pure, lovely, Spirit-filled thoughts.

- *Exhale* anxiety. *Inhale* patience.

- *Exhale* despair. *Inhale* the Holy Spirit as your companion.

- *Exhale* fear. *Inhale* God beside you.

- *Exhale* insecurity. *Inhale* confidence in God.

- *Breathe in* the Holy Spirit of God, the strength of God, the wisdom of God, and the heart of God. *Breathe out* anything else.

8-14

DAY 11 CHALLENGE

The apostle Paul gave clear instruction on how to live the Spirit-filled life. Even in the twenty-first century, his counsel remains relevant to every man and woman:

> When you follow the desires of your sinful nature, the results are very clear: sexual immorality, impurity, lustful pleasures, idolatry, sorcery, hostility, quarreling, jealousy, outbursts of anger, selfish ambition, dissension, division, envy, drunkenness, wild parties, and other sins like these. Let me tell you again, as I have before, that anyone living that sort of life will not inherit the Kingdom of God.
>
> But the Holy Spirit produces this kind of fruit in our lives: love, joy, peace, patience, kindness, goodness,

faithfulness, gentleness, and self-control. There is no law against these things!

Those who belong to Christ Jesus have nailed the passions and desires of their sinful nature to his cross and crucified them there. Since we are living by the Spirit, let us follow the Spirit's leading in every part of our lives. (Galatians 5:19–25)

Consider the following two questions. Try to be as transparent and honest as possible. I encourage you to be sincere and specific, so that you will receive more insight and power from God to live by His Spirit.

1. What destructive, negative, tempting thoughts do I need to breathe out of my life daily?

2. As I breathe in the Holy Spirit, what new thoughts and directions is He giving to me?

purified by fire

DAY 12:
SET APART

My husband became a pastoral counselor several years ago. His empathy and compassion and wisdom to help others "right" their sinking ships was born out of his personal pain and brokenness, which led him to Christ in his mid-twenties. Roger is a wonderful reflection of the God who lifts people out of despair and not only gives them new lives, but calls them to help others who are hurting, or lost, or struggling.

In the last decade, Roger's job is increasingly consumed with helping longtime Christians who are desperately struggling to break free from addictions to alcohol and sexual immorality. They often come to him utterly broken and needing to clean up after escapades of adultery or pornography.

Roger and I both came to Christ in the 1970s after hitting rock bottom. And because we inflicted so much pain and humiliation upon ourselves before coming to Christ, we fought against the desires and opportunities to return to or embrace our ungodly habits or haunts after becoming Christians.

I can't explain why, but those who come to Christ after a humiliating, shameful, wild, or worldly crash and burn, don't usually seem offended by requests from God and others to live "set apart" or different than everyone else. Or maybe I *can* explain it: they don't need to be convinced that they *should* live pure and moral lives—having already led impure and immoral lives, they vividly understand the results of self-destructive behavior and choices! In fact, people like Roger and me not only feel grateful for the call to step out of their shameful ways, but they're honored by the opportunity to live in ways that are right and pure and good.

So as singles and new Christians, Roger and I began working together for a student organization that required us to willingly abstain from alcohol and remain sexually pure (whether single or married). It was actually a very safe environment for me, minimizing the temptation to drink while providing great accountability and fun.

We began spending almost every weekend with teenagers: bowling, going to the beach, roller-skating, ice-skating, rock-climbing, hiking, rappelling, water-skiing, snow-skiing, and snowmobiling. Our lives were packed with action—and lots of fast food! We always laughed. There was always something adventurous or exciting or meaningful going on, and we knew we were making a lasting impact on the lives of hundreds of students every year.

We have the greatest memories . . . and after working together for only one year, Roger asked me to marry him, before we had ever even kissed or dated! I said yes, and for more than twenty-seven years we have enjoyed great happiness in our marriage, family life, work, and recreation. Though no one ever asked us to agree in writing, Roger and I have remained committed to sobriety and fidelity (and even bowling), just like when we were youth workers!

Our new way of living was wonderfully fulfilling and adventurous. We attributed so much of our joy to the fact that we were getting rid of the old ways of living! We were committed to honoring God by living as pure and holy as we could.

8-14

Leviticus 11:45 is one of the first verses in the Bible that speaks about holiness. It says, "I, the LORD, am the one who brought you up from the land of Egypt, that I might be your God. Therefore, you must be holy because I am holy." This is the Old Testament passage that Paul refers to in 1 Peter 1:15–16, when he speaks boldly to every believer: "Now you must be holy in everything you do, just as God who chose you is holy. For the Scriptures say, 'You must be holy because I am holy.'"

In Hendrickson Publishers' *The Pulpit Commentary* on Leviticus, holiness is given two focuses. The first describes holiness as a "divine call." God calls us and delivers us out of our old lives to be His, set apart and holy. It is a privilege to be called by God, to have an intimate relationship with Him, and to be chosen by and uniquely set apart for Him. The commentary goes on to explain: "A redeemed life must be holy. We begin our holiness with the Cross of Christ. He has cleansed us with his blood, therefore we must be clean." As we mature, the call to holiness means that "likeness to God is our rule."[28]

The second focus in *The Pulpit Commentary* on Leviticus discussed the method of holiness. How are we to live and be holy? "The holiness which God requires is personal holiness—holiness in life, manners, habits, food, everything which concerns the man himself." And "holiness must be the characteristic of God's people as a community."[29]

Yet, if we are completely honest, we see a twenty-first-century church looking about the same as the rest of society. Frankly, so many Christians seem comfortable living lives that resemble the world!

One reason Christians struggle with living holy lives could be cultural. Society is more permissive: daytime and evening television is practically devoid of morality, and social gatherings of every kind feel incomplete without hard liquors, beer, and wine for the guests. And movies inundate us with sexual content and vulgar language. Fewer and fewer options exist for set apart, yet abundantly full and exciting lives!

Sadly, believers allow others to set the standard for their lives.

But God has not called you and me to be like others. He has called you and me to be like Him; and He is holy!

The entire focus of the Fellowship of the Burning Heart in 1947 was to live differently than the world, to live by the Word of God, and to impact the world for God. They were convinced that living sober and pure lives would set them apart in a world that was loveless, lustful, and longing for truth. But they were equally convinced that they must live holy lives with joy and conviction, rather than with resentment or bitterness.

Those with burning hearts should leave a lasting, enticing, appealing impression on others. People with burning hearts are filled and overflowing with a contagious fire of love and power and purity. They have been through the refiner's fire and have come out pure and glowing. They brilliantly reflect the God they serve.

DAY 12 CHALLENGE

8-14

It is so easy to be duped into thinking that outbursts of anger, unplanned sexual encounters, getting buzzed, or being involved with pornography are just part of life.

If you hear yourself saying, "Everyone else is doing it" or, "It's not that clear-cut" or, "It's not hurting anyone," it is time to more clearly define your lifestyle in comparison to God's Word.

What are the specific areas in your life in which you refuse to be set apart?

Just as the Fellowship of the Burning Heart defined "holy living" for their lives, I encourage you to meditate on 1 Peter 1:15–16: "Now you must be holy in everything you do, just as God who chose you is holy. For the Scriptures say, 'You must be holy because I am holy.'" Define how holiness—moral blamelessness—can be a part of your life.

DAY 13:
THE COST OF A
BURNING HEART

For more than twenty years, without ever seeing or knowing about the Fellowship of the Burning Heart, I have felt compelled by the Holy Spirit to make lifelong commitments to one hour a day in prayer, fidelity in my marriage, sobriety, and sharing my faith in Christ with all who will listen!

Yet, in my pursuit of a burning heart, I have encountered many barriers. Some of these have actually come from those I would have expected to encourage and support my commitments.

For example, when I made a decision in 1984 to pray one hour a day and then call students to the same, other leaders in ministry struggled with my "call to prayer." In fact, I even remember where I was standing when one of my supervisors came up to me and suggested that I never mention to anyone that I pray an hour a day because it might sound prideful. The last thing I had in mind was pride! I needed (and still need) prayer to survive!

I was impressionable, looking for advice. So I delved into stacks of books on prayer written by many of the "greats" (such as George Muller, Leonard Ravenhill, and Andrew Murray), only to find that they too were called by God to a similar, if not greater, commitment of time in prayer. And guess what? They called other believers to join in as well.

Years later, I worked on a traveling youth team, and I once again suggested calling students to one hour in prayer. I wanted so badly to share the power available in prayer with students. I knew an hour with God was the discipline I needed to stay . . .

on fire,

aware of my weaknesses,

regularly humbled, and

in love and connected with Him.

But the team thought it was a far too time-consuming and guilt-producing discipline to ask students to consider. Their rejection of my idea made me feel—true or untrue—as if they considered me legalistic. One thing I continue to learn about possessing a burning heart: if God calls you to deeper levels of prayer, purity, and purpose, you might be misunderstood as legalistic and will often stand alone.

Possessing a heart that burns to be holy like God is costly. Charles Spurgeon preached much about the Holy Spirit to believers who were negligent about holiness in their lives. He begged believers to see the correlation between holiness and effective Christian lives. In one of his sermons he said, "It is important that we be under the influence of the Holy Ghost as he is the Spirit of holiness; for a very considerable and essential part of Christian ministry lies in example."[30]

Spurgeon continued, "May you also possess the grand moral characteristic of courage. By this we do not mean impertinence, impudence, or self-conceit, but real courage to do and say calmly the right thing, and to go straight on at all hazards, though there should be none to give you a good word. I am astonished at the number of Christians who are afraid to speak the truth to their brethren."[31]

It wasn't just my commitment to prayer that elicited tension. In the areas of sobriety and purity, I have always felt God call me to live by standards that were not asked of me by any teacher, church, or pastor. In fact, in almost thirty years, I have rarely attended any fellowship where I was told how to act or was called to make commitments of moral purity, abstinence, or sobriety.

But just as God called those in the Fellowship of the Burning Heart, He called me, my husband, and many others to commit to living sober, sexually pure lives since the beginning of our Christian walk.

Years ago, I became a part of an organization that made presentations to hundreds of youth groups. At each event, I shared my story with the students that as a binge-drinking teenager I became a suicidal alcoholic, until God dramatically changed my life.

After the events, the team always went out to dinner. I was new to the group, so the first time I arrived at the restaurant, I was speechless when I approached the long table with more alcoholic beverages on it than I'd seen since my party days.

I didn't know what to say. I felt really uncomfortable. My first thought was, *Here I am speaking to students about abstinence, and I am in the middle of more alcohol than food!* If the people who heard me speak about being a recovered alcoholic came into the restaurant and saw me sitting there, would they be able to tell that none of the alcoholic drinks were mine? Would they have the courage to ask me? And what if seeing the beers caused them to consider me either a liar or hypocrite? And what if they spread that word around? Or worse yet, what if someone gave up in his or her own battle for sobriety because of seeing me in this scene?

Thoughts and questions flooded my mind.

I know the Bible does not say, "Do not drink." But it does say in Proverbs 20:1, "Wine is a mocker and beer a brawler; whoever is led astray by them is not wise" (NIV). And Proverbs 23:31–32 says, "Do not gaze at wine when it is red, when it sparkles in the cup, when it goes down smoothly! In the end it bites like a snake and poisons like a viper" (NIV).

It is both my observation and life experience that alcohol and sex are often attracted to each other. What if I, due either to the pressure to fit in or being exposed to so much alcohol, had taken a drink after fifteen years of sobriety because of the overwhelming temptation? Doing so would have absolutely broken my longstanding sobriety boundaries that night with fellow ministers and possibly put me in a position to cross sexual boundaries as well.

At first, I refused even to sit at the table. I asked to speak with my immediate boss and requested permission not to attend the dinners. He felt that I should tell the team, in our very next meeting, why I would not be at the dinners.

Leading up to the next meeting, I felt uncomfortable, embarrassed, ashamed, and stupid. This was going to be very difficult, but I had to share my heart, knowing that I would possibly increase the impression that I was ultraconservative or extremely legalistic. But most importantly, I felt I had to stand for and make known my convictions even in a setting of fellow ministers. At the meeting, I took some really deep breaths, and while holding back tears, I told them my struggle. After I shared my concerns with the team, I was both surprised and relieved that the standing policy among the team members was not to drink when I was present. I was extremely grateful for the team's willingness to respond to me with love and respect, putting aside their freedoms on my behalf.

In the name of freedom, we have to consider whether our actions are hurting or undermining the faith, or even the morality of others. We must ask ourselves, "Are my actions contributing positively or negatively to those who struggle with alcohol abuse or sexual purity in a culture that is rampant with binge drinking, alcohol addiction, sexual immorality, and adultery? Am I aware of the boundaries, especially sexual boundaries, that are often broken when people drink? Do I see my life reflecting the world or the Word?"

The cost of a burning heart is being willing to stand firm, even to stand alone in areas of prayer, purity, and purpose.

DAY 13 CHALLENGE

Friends, we have a great message to bring to a world that is looking for a loving, powerful, personal God. As His messengers, our lives must reflect the message we bring. Do you desire to be a messenger of the good news?

Paul reminded the Thessalonians, "Our gospel came to you not simply with words, but also with power, with the Holy Spirit and with deep conviction. You know how we lived among you for your sake" (1 Thessalonians 1:5 NIV).

The apostle Peter said, "It is God's will that your honorable lives should silence those ignorant people who make foolish accusations against you. For you are free, yet you are God's slaves, so don't use your freedom as an excuse to do evil" (1 Peter 2:15–16).

And Paul, in speaking to the Ephesians, wrote, "Be careful how you live. Don't live like fools, but like those who are wise. Make the most of every opportunity in these evil days. Don't act thoughtlessly, but understand what the Lord wants you to do. Don't be drunk with wine, because that will ruin your life. Instead, be filled with the Holy Spirit" (Ephesians 5:15–18).

Is it possible that the Holy Spirit is asking you to consider changing an area of your life to more powerfully reflect the holiness of the God you serve?

Have a written conversation with God today—whether you are struggling or standing alone.

8-14

purified by fire

DAY 14:
HOLINESS IS NOT
AN OPTION

Holiness is simply not an option with God. His Word and His call to purity are clear and unchanging.

In *The Pursuit of Holiness*, Jerry Bridges makes a very honest assessment of the struggle to understand the role of holiness in a believer's life. First, he discusses the misconceptions of holiness. "In some circles, holiness is equated with a series of prohibitions. . . . For others, holiness means a particular style of dress and mannerisms. For still others, it means unattainable perfection, an idea that fosters either delusion or discouragement about one's sin. All of these ideas, while accurate to some degree, miss the true concept. To be holy is to be morally blameless."[32]

If holiness has always been clearly defined, perhaps the more prominent reason believers are so uncomfortable with holiness is that they are unfamiliar with the Word of God.

In *The Holy Spirit*, Billy Graham discusses the stark contrast between the ways of the flesh and the ways of holiness. He uses

Galatians 5 to present the lifestyle of one who is possessed by Christ:

> So I say, live by the Spirit, and you will not gratify the desires of the sinful nature. For the sinful nature desires what is contrary to the Spirit, and the Spirit what is contrary to sinful nature. They are in conflict with each other. . . . The acts of the sinful nature are obvious: sexual immorality, impurity, and debauchery; idolatry and witchcraft, hatred, discord, jealousy, fits of rage, selfish ambition, dissensions, factions and envy, drunkenness, orgies, and the like. (Galatians 5:16–20 NIV)

But this is not the only place in Scripture where lists of sins are given. Colossians 3:3–5 reads:

> For you died to this life, and your real life is hidden with Christ in God. And when Christ, who is your life, is revealed to the whole world, you will share in all his glory. So put to death the sinful, earthly things lurking within you. Have nothing to do with sexual immorality, impurity, lust, and evil desires. Don't be greedy, for a greedy person is an idolater, worshiping the things of this world.

If the Word of God makes the recognition of unholy lifestyles so obvious, then why don't we see more walking, breathing, professing, and holy Christians?

Billy Graham made another interesting observation in his book *The Holy Spirit* that I continue to find relevant nearly three decades later: "Today people do many of these forbidden things in the name of freedom. What they fail to see is that such activities actually enslave those who become involved in them. True freedom consists not in the freedom to sin, but the freedom not to sin."[33]

Maybe we just don't want to call sin in our lives what it is— sin!

In his book *Heart After God,* Luis Palau writes, "Immorality begins with tiny things. Little things. Yet, if you don't crucify them, if you don't bring them to judgment, if you don't face up to them for what they are—sin—they can destroy you. They can blur your moral judgment at a critical, irreversible juncture in your life. No one sees the little flaws, but everyone sees the big collapse."[34]

There is another reason for lack of both personal and community holiness: the lack of regular examination of our lives before God and others.

Are you in the habit of confessing your sins corporately or privately, even in writing? Do you *daily* identify and agree with God about the areas of your life that God calls sin? (The previous lists in Galatians 5 and Colossians 3 can give us a lot of insight.) Do you daily ask for God's help to steer clear of the areas in which you struggle? Do you tolerate unconfessed sin in your life? Are you willing to be accountable to others regarding any areas of struggle? Are you willing to make written commitments to change or to stop?

Whether you are a young or mature Christian, Jerry Bridges is quick to remind us that holiness is not a condition of coming to Christ. Yet he also reminds us, "Therefore, we may say that no one can trust in Christ for true salvation unless he trusts in Him for holiness. This does not mean the desire for holiness must be a conscious desire at the time a person comes to Christ, but rather that the Holy Spirit who creates in us a saving faith also creates within us the desire for holiness. He simply does not create one without the other."[35]

Holiness is absolutely achievable in our lives when we know what God's Word says about it, when we are convinced that God has called us to it, and when we are willing to daily examine ourselves in front of Him.

Holiness reflected in an entire community will start a contagious fire! People looking for hope and longing to be loved are drawn closer to God when they encounter those whose hearts burn brightly in reflection of Him.

Purity is an essential component of a burning heart. Paul wrote in 2 Timothy 2:21, "If you keep yourself pure, you will be a special utensil for honorable use. Your life will be clean, and you will be ready for the Master to use you for every good work"!

When you're purified by fire, you'll be ablaze with purpose.

DAY 14 CHALLENGE

Paul called believers to lead by example. In Titus 2:7, he wrote, "You yourself must be an example to them by doing good works of every kind. Let everything you do reflect the integrity and seriousness of your teaching."

I believe God is calling, looking for people who will live pure and holy lives for Him, who will take the gift and power of His *Holy* Spirit to the masses.

Today, I encourage you to ask a few friends to share in an honest conversation. Examine your lives in front of each other. Ask if they see any area in your life that might hinder the reflection of a holy God. Provide a safe place for confidential confession and prayer. Ask them to consider becoming accountability partners for you and for each other. Continue to meet in prayer for each other.

Start your own Burning Hearts Club with people who are also committed to reflecting the holiness of God by the way you live!

8-14

ABLAZE WITH PURPOSE

Do you ever wonder if your life really matters? It does! Sociologists tell us that "the most introverted of people will influence 10,000 others in an average lifetime."[36]

If you possess a burning heart for God, it will not only change your life, but it will ultimately impact, influence, and inspire countless others for eternity.

The final component in the written contract of the 1947 Fellowship of the Burning Heart was forged out of the members' desire to burn so intensely with the love of God and be so fueled by the supernatural power of His Holy Spirit that those whom they encountered would, in fact, encounter *God*. Their signed commitment was to introduce at least one person to Christ each year.

They believed it was every man and woman's purpose to bring glory to God by being completely available to Him with their lives. And though they recognized they were each equipped with different and specific spiritual gifts, they counted it a privilege to stand by the door where seekers could enter to find eternal life.

That night at the campground, they were set ablaze! They were "on fire" and called to boldly reach an entire country of college students with the good news of Jesus Christ.

The members of the Fellowship of the Burning Heart were convinced that if they did not allow anything to extinguish their fire, they were unstoppable. Therefore, they carefully put concrete form to their convictions and passion through this pledge, knowing that the task was too huge to accomplish on their own.

During that world-changing night of prayer, they understood the gravity of their contract. It was preparation for a movement of the Holy Spirit.

In the next seven days, as you consider the call upon and purpose for your life, I challenge you not to look past anyone or assume what someone has already decided about God. Show them who He is and how He loves.

You don't just have *what* they want; you have *Who* they want!

ablaze with purpose

DAY 15:
REPRESENT YOUR
FATHER

As teenagers, just before we left the house, my dad would always say, "Remember, you represent the Hunter family." It was definitely a ploy to get us to think about our plans for the evening and to consider making any adjustments before doing something that might embarrass ourselves or the family name.

The day I became a Christian, the janitor, though not exactly using my dad's words, explained that believers are called to represent God. Much like an ambassador represents his or her country, Christians are called to be ambassadors who represent Christ.

The janitor read 2 Corinthians 5:17–20 not only to convince me that I was new and saved, but also to send me out:

> This means that anyone who belongs to Christ has become a new person. The old life is gone; a new life has begun!
>
> And all of this is a gift from God, who brought us

back to himself through Christ. And God has given us this task of reconciling people to him. For God was in Christ, reconciling the world to himself, no longer counting people's sins against them. And he gave us this wonderful message of reconciliation. So we are Christ's ambassadors; God is making his appeal through us. We speak for Christ when we plead, "Come back to God!"

I've always believed that 2 Corinthians 5:17–20 encapsulates the true call of every believer. First, you become a brand-new person when you are reconciled to God through Christ's death on the cross. This promised transformation in your life becomes a testimony of God's love and power. Then without further delay, you are immediately entrusted with a mission to be an ambassador of the living, loving God. You are a spokesperson for Him, an influencer who has the authority to take the gospel message to others.

I really felt the weight of that passage in my life as a new believer. I am amazed at the janitor's courage in calling me to such responsibility! Yet, in many ways, he set my life on a course destined for leadership.

I had such a horrible reputation that most mentors might have suggested I stay quiet about my experience with God until my life was more presentable. But instead, the church janitor encouraged me to live like I believed I was a child of the King.

He impressed upon me that my actions—from that moment forward—would either have a negative or positive effect on *God's* reputation, not just my own.

Before the Holy Spirit came into my life, my lack of moral and ethical character was evident to my bosses, co-workers, friends, and family. So it seemed rather logical that if I went back to work after becoming a Christian and told people how much God loved me and forgave me and changed me, yet I continued with my filthy habits, I would not be taken seriously. Most importantly, I would not represent my Father well.

Truthfully, I was more than willing to get rid of my shameful reputation. I was thrilled with my new title: ambassador of the King! It gave me something to live for and kept me moving forward instead of looking back. I was determined to be a credible representative of God. With the indwelling power of the Holy Spirit upholding my "Second Corinthians commissioning," I had supernatural courage and a real incentive to live differently in front of others.

14-21

Mind you, I wasn't in an official ministry capacity. I hadn't even identified my spiritual gifts. I only knew that I carried the Holy Spirit of the living God within me, and I had a responsibility to share Him with anyone and everyone. The impression and call of this assignment—which I received from God almost thirty years ago—has never faded!

Whether you come to God in pretty good shape or a total mess, 2 Corinthians 5:17–20 is designed to give you instant momentum and motivation. Because God loves, forgives, and fills you with power to change, you are no longer the same person. You have Someone to please and represent!

I am suggesting that anyone who is a child of the King should humbly accept the role of ambassador. And with that assignment, I encourage you to commit every facet of your life to the highest standards of leadership and service.

Being an ambassador of the King is a lifelong position. From your first day as a believer until your last day on earth, you represent God—you are His messenger, His reconciler, and His ambassador!

DAY 15 CHALLENGE

Make a list of the people with whom you regularly come into contact. Begin with your inner circle of family, and then move out to neighbors, friends, and co-workers. Remember that your sphere of influence also includes acquaintances, passersby, store clerks, bank tellers, and even strangers.

Begin a section in your prayer notebook that lists their names (with space under each name). During the next year, ask God to give you His heart for these people. Write down and follow up on any thoughts He gives you regarding each person. Invite them to meetings, events, concerts, or church services that you know might be of particular interest to them.

Consider each encounter you have with these people as taking them one step closer to God. Be genuine and Spirit-led in your conversations. And if your friends or co-workers or family members aren't open to your invitations, don't take it personally. Continue to humbly do the work of an ambassador!

14-21

DAY 16:
DON'T EXTINGUISH
THE FIRE

Recently, I felt encouraged by the Holy Spirit to do something unusual—but it took a little prodding.

It began with a thought to leave a meeting a bit early and stop at my favorite frozen yogurt shop on my way home. Actually, that thought doesn't require a lot of prodding, but I was in a huge hurry to get home because there was something I really wanted to do by a certain time.

So I slipped out of the meeting, convinced that I could still "beat the clock" if I rushed right in and got right out of the store.

The closer I got to the yogurt shop, the more anxious I became about the time. But when it was too late to turn toward home without turning around, I made a mad dash for the best parking spot and quickly got in line at the counter.

One of the clerks with whom I always chat seemed very red-eyed and sad. I knew that if I acknowledged her sadness, it might delay my quick escape. Nevertheless, it would have been rude of me not to ask, "How are you?" So I did, reluctantly.

Without hesitation, she told me three very sad things that had happened during the day. With tears welling up in her eyes, she added, "And today is my birthday." I knew that both her parents had recently died, and I was pretty sure she didn't really have any other family, or for that matter, many friends.

I couldn't think of any response that would help her except, "I'll pray for you." I was so preoccupied with my schedule that I didn't even wish her, "Happy Birthday."

As I left the shop and walked to my car, I chided myself. *That was really poor. What were you thinking? How is telling her that you'll pray for her going to make her feel happy right now?*

When the following thought popped into my head, I knew God had entered the conversation. *What can you do, Becky, to make her birthday feel happy?*

Well, I thought, *I can drive to the drugstore and buy her a card. But that will take time. My yogurt will melt, and I'll get home later than I wanted.* Yet I had a very strong impression that God had something for me to do that could give a hurting person a very real sense of His presence, if I would just put aside my plans.

By the time I got to the shopping center, my thoughts changed from just "buying a card" to "buying a card and a little gift" and then to "finding a perfect card and a really nice, memorable gift."

I parked, got out of the car, and decided to go into the florist shop rather than the drug store. There were dozens of nice, small, affordable plants. But they just didn't seem special.

So I kept looking around. The bouquets of flowers were much prettier, but when my eyes caught a dozen roses of *twelve different colors*, I knew I had found the perfect gift.

Then I looked at the price. They were beautiful but expensive! By this point, time and money became irrelevant. I was sure that God had me on a mission. He was looking and waiting for someone in this clerk's life to give her a gift from Him *today*, and fortunately, when He began putting His thoughts into my mind, I recognized His voice, reluctantly acknowledged it, ignored my selfishness, and responded to His request.

While the flowers were being prepared in a vase and travel carton, I searched for the perfect card. Without hesitating, I began to write words I believed God was giving me: "God asked me to wish you a happy birthday and to give you these flowers on His behalf. He wanted me to remind you to talk to Him. He is there for you; He is listening. Your friend, Becky."

I packed up the vase of roses and drove back to the yogurt shop with real excitement! After noticing the excruciating sadness in the clerk's eyes on the first visit, I couldn't wait to see her face this time! Just the thought that God might use me to bring this woman some happiness tipped me over the edge, and I determined to make it a full-blown ordeal and sing "Happy Birthday" as I entered the front doors . . . for all to hear!

After handing her the flowers and card, I heard a customer remark, "Oh, what a great friend you have!" I thought, *I don't even know this woman's last name . . . but God does! And yes, He's a great friend!*

14-21

This time I saw tears of joy welling up in the clerk's eyes. As she read the card, all she could say was, "I'm overwhelmed." I said through my own tears, "I am too!" Then I added, "God really loves you. He wants you to know that. He wants you to talk to Him."

She asked, "Can I hug you?"

As I hugged her, I whispered in her ear, "I, too, have been desperate and in huge emotional pain. I've even been suicidal. But you're not alone. God is there for you. He wants you to talk to Him."

I simply couldn't ignore God's prompting on my life that night. I felt Him as powerfully over me in those few minutes as I do when speaking for crowds of thousands.

Day in and day out,

    moment by moment,

      hour after hour,

God gives us thoughts, ideas, and words to say. *He* prompts us to go, do, and be Him to those around us. It may be a serious or prophetic word you are to speak to someone. It might be a simple gesture or a small act of kindness.

Galatians 5:25 says, "Since we are living by the Spirit, let us follow the Spirit's leading in every part of our lives."

Don't compartmentalize the Holy Spirit once He enters your life! He desires to lead you in every area, action, thought, and word. He does so by instructing you through your thoughts, your quiet time, and even through physical symptoms, such as a pounding heart. You may not even have to speak a word, but He wants you to encourage, lift, love, and draw others to Him. You must be looking and listening for His voice and impressions.

You don't want to miss out on the excitement or the privilege of being a janitor or a delivery person or the one who brings a healing touch to one of His children.

DAY 16 CHALLENGE

First Thessalonians 5:19 says, "Do not put out the Spirit's fire" (NIV)!

Many of us tend to extinguish the fire of the Holy Spirit in our lives by ignoring His promptings or not recognizing His voice. We miss out on so much of the supernatural action and overwhelming joy that happens when we are involved in doing what God wants to us to do! But I am equally convinced that we, as parents and spouses and friends, are equally guilty of putting out the Spirit's fire in those around us.

Be careful. Pray before speaking. If God has called someone to do something radical or different or daring, you must not extinguish or throw water on the Holy Spirit's fire in them by critical, negative, or discouraging words.

Today, be on the lookout to fill someone's needs. Be aware. Pay attention! Many families need someone to make a meal for them, older neighbors often need rides to appointments, young

14-21

couples would love to have someone watch their kids while they spend a quiet dinner out, and family members often need help with projects. Act on any thoughts of kindness that cross your mind; don't just think about them—do them!

DAY 17:
ANOINTED TO DO

My mother is an eighty-three-year-old phenom. She plays golf three or four times a week, has a 27 handicap, but often shoots in the 90s and regularly wins a few skins!

Mom grew up in the Depression and struggled with her identity as a child of an immigrant. As a young woman, she made her own clothes and became a fabulous seamstress. She was married fifty-four years (until my dad died), is a mother of three, and worked until she was seventy-five as an interior decorator. She paints with oils, takes weekly organ lessons, and is a great cook and a born leader (or very bossy, however you want to look at it!).

She has always, since I was a child, had a very real concern for the homeless, poor, and hungry. One of my earliest memories is driving to a rural area to deliver food and clothes (not items from a food bank but things she collected from our house) to a church family who was down-and-out.

In fact, the year my father died, my mother still lived in

Cleveland and all the kids lived in California. She decided to stay home that year and spend Christmas Day serving food with the Salvation Army to the homeless in downtown Cleveland. She knew that most people with families tend not to volunteer on actual holidays. So my mom enthusiastically filled the gap!

To this day, she drives neighbors to their doctors' appointments and always—and I mean always—delivers a dinner or a fruit plate if she hears someone in her neighborhood isn't feeling well. Her ability to serve with compassion is amazing.

Recently she came to my house to dog-sit my Labrador retriever for a few days. She also volunteered to complete a collation project for me while she was there, which saved my company hundreds of dollars.

I called at one point to check in, and my mom said, "I'm finished with the project. Do you have anything else for me to do?" She is wired to serve!

When I returned from the weekend retreat, Mom excitedly asked, "Did I tell you what happened at my outreach center last week?"

I said, "What outreach center?" I had no idea my mom volunteered every Friday at a food center near her home, helping families who need groceries and possible emergency housing.

She continued, "They've asked me to learn the computer and enter information; so I'm either at the front desk or I stand at the food distribution counter. Last week, a young woman came into the center and approached me at the front desk. Before I could stop her, she poured out the saddest series of events that caused her to lose her job, get an eviction notice from her landlord, and accumulate medical bills that she couldn't pay. In addition, she had no food or money and her car repeatedly broke down. She was crying uncontrollably. She was so desperate that I actually feared she might do something to harm herself."

Mom went on to say, "As the woman was speaking, I realized that our center was not really equipped to help her. Her needs were so great and she was so desperate, I couldn't just turn her away without something more. So I said a little prayer and asked God what I could do to help her.

"The next thing I knew, a boldness came over me and I told her to drive to a church in our community that might truly be able to help her. I told her to go there right away, today! Then I said, 'I want you to tell the people the *exact* story you just told me.'"

The woman left.

One week later, the woman returned to the outreach center and asked to speak with my mom. She said, "You won't believe what happened. I did just what you told me. I went to that church, and I begged. I even told them I felt bad about begging, but the woman on the other side of the counter told me that it was their honor to help me! And they did. They called the doctor and had my medical bills waived. They found another doctor to treat my current condition. They had a lawyer call my landlord and ask for an extension until I get a job. They found someone to fix my car for free, and they are

14-21

training me to get a job in another field."

My mother has the spiritual gift of service. And she has used it all of her life! When she didn't have help for that woman, she directed her to a place where she would get help.

Every believer is given a spiritual gift for the purpose of using it to help others and to serve God. These gifts aren't given to us just to enjoy for ourselves!

In the wildly successful *The Purpose Driven Life*, Rick Warren, pastor of Saddleback Church, gives an easy formula for understanding the purpose for which you were born. He says, "You were *shaped* to serve God. Before God created you, he decided what role he wanted you to play on earth. He planned exactly how he wanted you to serve him, and then he shaped you for those tasks. You are the way you are because you were made for a specific ministry."[37]

Through a series of days in his book, Warren teaches the SHAPE method, which gives us five factors to discover and use our lives to serve God:

Spiritual gifts

Heart

Abilities

Personality

Experience

The story about my mother is a perfect illustration of the gift of service that God gave my mother—decades ago—and she has never hesitated to use it. In addition to her gift, God gave my mother a very bold personality, which directed the gal to the church . . . *right then* and there! I believe God wanted to help her right then, and He needed someone to point her to the exact place where her needs would be met. And because of my mom's painful experience of growing up in the Depression, she has a real heart for the homeless and hungry! At eighty-three, she is compelled to serve God. And, wow, did she make a dramatic difference in someone's life that day!

DAY 17 CHALLENGE

In 1 Corinthians 12, Paul gives a thorough teaching on the gifts of the Spirit. He says, "Now there are different kinds of spiritual gifts, but it is the same Holy Spirit who is the source of them all. There are different kinds of service in the church, but it is the same Lord we are serving" (v. 4 NIV). Then Paul lists several kinds of spiritual gifts:

> To one there is given through the Spirit the message of wisdom, to another the message of knowledge by means of the same Spirit, to another faith by the same Spirit, to another gifts of healing by that one Spirit, to another miraculous powers, to another prophecy, to another distinguishing between spirits, to another speaking in different kinds of tongues, and to still another the interpretation of tongues. All these are the work of one and the same Spirit, and he gives them to each one, just as he determines. (vv. 8–11 NIV)

14-21

If you are uncertain of your spiritual gift, do not hesitate to discover more about all of the gifts, especially yours! Don't waste any more time! Buy a few books on the gifts of the Holy Spirit. Cross-reference verses in the Bible on the gifts of the Spirit, take an on-line test, and dig in! You are meant to use your spiritual gift your entire life! You are never too old (or too young) to serve God.

DAY 18:
STAND BY THE DOOR

By now, you've probably assessed one of my spiritual gifts. No, it is not the gift of gab! I have the spiritual gift of evangelism.

To this day, I'm perfectly comfortable talking to strangers about God. I always tell the story about how God changed my life to anyone who will listen! I love sharing with seatmates on cross-country flights, with people riding in hotel elevators, and with servers in restaurants. In fact, on a recent flight, my co-worker and I were seated one directly behind the other, rather than side-by-side. When we deplaned, she said, "I timed you." I asked, "What do you mean?" She said, "It only took you twenty minutes before you shared your story with the lady next to you. I even fell asleep . . . and you were still talking when I woke up!"

Why am I so open about God when many people are so quiet about their relationship with Him? Because I realize that if the janitor had looked at me on my most desperate day and thought, *She's probably never going to change; she couldn't possibly want*

God in her life since she's involved in the exact opposite lifestyle—I might not be alive today!

Because of this, I have an ongoing mission in my life never to miss an opportunity to connect someone to the living, loving God. I am living proof that you never know if people are genuinely interested or in need of God's power or presence until you talk to them. Their outward appearance or even their present circumstances will keep you guessing . . . and you could be wrong!

Presenting God to others as Someone who is relevant and loving and able to meet their needs should be a compelling desire in all of our lives. I believe that introducing people to God is one of the most important things we are here on earth to do—and not just if you have the gift of evangelism! We must each have a true and burning desire to make a difference in people's lives by connecting them to God, knowing that it will impact them both now and for eternity!

A favorite poem of mine that captures the passion of a person who is compelled to connect people to God. A brief excerpt from *I Stand by the Door*, by Samuel Shoemaker, presents the position of one who knows God and can't help but lead others to Him:

> I stand by the door.
> I neither go too far in, nor stay too far out,
> The door is the most important door in the world—

It is the door through which men walk when they find
    God.
There's no use my going way inside, and staying there,
When so many are still outside and they, as much as I,
Crave to know where the door is.

The most tremendous thing in the world
Is for men to find that door—the door to God.
The most important thing any man can do
Is to take hold of one of those blind, groping hands,
And put it on the latch—the latch that only clicks
and opens to the man's own touch.[38]

As a youth worker, I ministered to students of various ages and backgrounds and races. But there was one common need: they all needed God's love. Their lives seemed to revolve around some drama that kept spinning them out of control, and though they were masters at communicating with friends, they were equally savvy at ignoring parents and avoiding God!

I believed if I could connect students with God—especially if I never saw them again—then, for the rest of their lives, these young people would always be in His hands. Sometimes it took months just to help them understand God's love, and it took even more time and patience to show them how to *stay* connected to Him! Though most of the high school students with whom I worked were hesitant and fragile and indecisive, I never had a desire to leave the doorway.

Later in Shoemaker's poem, he discusses those folks who go too far inside the door and forget about the people outside. He says:

> As for me, I shall take my old accustomed place,
> near enough to God to hear Him, and know He is there,
> but not so far from men as not to hear them,
> and remember they are there, too.[39]

It takes great tenacity to keep standing and waiting at the door for those who continually disappoint us.

It takes great humility to stand at the door and not judge another.

It takes great self-control not to criticize another.

It takes great kindness to lovingly look at the unlovely and welcome them with your smile and handshake.

It takes great maturity to understand how fortunate you are not to be in their shoes.

It takes great contentment to wait for a new face to come by instead of wandering from the door for something more fun, convenient, or comfortable.

It takes great commitment to stand by a cold door rather than sit and enjoy your friends' company inside.

Standing by the door is not an option for those who have a burning heart. It is a privilege, a response. It should well be the passion of everyone who knows the living, loving God to make

Him known to others, but not for the purpose of winning people to our side or way of thinking. No, connecting people to God is offering them real life, unconditional love, an eternal future, and hope for today!

Wesley Duewel challenges us: "Do you long to be a person of God with such a passion for souls that God begins to add a new dimension of fruitfulness to your leadership? Dare you believe that God will give it to you if you ask? Not everyone is called to be a Whitefield, a Billy Graham, or a Praying Hyde. But every one of us is called to bear fruit—both the fruit of the Spirit and the fruit of souls."[40]

DAY 18 CHALLENGE

We must remember that we possess the most life-changing presence and power available to man. And if we are convinced that people seek truth and long for love, then we can't be silent! We have what they want!

There is a door by which you and I are to stand every day. Stand attentively, look out at the passersby with attention and concern, put your hand out for theirs, and place their hand on the door.

Be prepared at all times to tell your story. As Paul wrote to Timothy, "Preach the word of God. Be prepared, whether the time is favorable or not" (2 Timothy 4:2).

Know how to tell your story of God's great love in one minute or in five minutes, over an afternoon or a weekend.

14-21

Never underestimate the hunger one might have to know your God. Never judge by appearance. Never assume.

If God sends someone—especially a stranger—your way, then your intervention or your invitation might be just what that person needs to be connected to God. In fact, I challenge you to pray for someone to come into your life this week.

DAY 19:
LOVE BOLDLY AND
OUTRAGEOUSLY

In the late 1990s, a book written one century earlier by Charles M. Sheldon reemerged in a new generation and set off a tidal wave of conviction . . . mixed with trendy marketing. (If you're familiar with *WWJD* bracelets, this is the book that inspired them.) Written in 1897, *In His Steps* struck twentieth-century believers with the same surge of passion intended by its author when it was first published.

In the fictional story, a transient homeless man wanders into a town. In just one short week, through his actions, questions, and unexpected death, the entire town is forced to re-examine their lifestyles and beliefs about God. The story unfolds in such a powerful way that all the town's citizens are challenged to live one year of their lives guided by the question: "What would Jesus do?" The compelling account of how people from every walk of life were changed by this challenge has lit fires in readers for well over a hundred years.

The question is relatively straightforward, but the answer

always seems to create a little tension. In every situation, Jesus would love *boldly* and *outrageously* and *radically*.

Not surprisingly, the courage to answer the question with specific actions creates a dilemma for most individuals, no matter the era. When we ask ourselves, "What would Jesus do?" fear can sometimes grip us. We are naturally inclined to ask ourselves, "What will it cost me? How much of my time or money will I have to give away? What must I change, give up, put aside, or stop doing in order to do what Jesus would do in my community, neighborhood, or home?" Our first response tends not to be, "How much or how often can I give or show love?"

Perhaps the key that unlocks our willingness and ability to love others is to understand Jesus's motives for loving.

Jesus loved others to please His Father. His love was so pure that the results of His intervention, healing, mercy, power, and grace always pointed back to God the Father. Jesus loved the unlovely. He spoke to the lonely. He ate with sinners. He mingled with social outcasts. He looked into the eyes of the ashamed. He had more friends who were unfortunate, sick, and rejected than friends who possessed earthly power or prestige.

Jesus also loved in order to show us the traits of His Father. He was empathetic, compassionate, forgiving, and understanding . . . even at the expense of being misunderstood by the religious.

Jesus did not simply love others in order to earn the respect of His observers. He lived—and loved—to please His Father and to demonstrate His Father's love for us.

When you and I struggle with how or when to love, I

believe there is only one way to settle the inner debate. We must identify with Jesus. We must see ourselves as He saw Himself—a sacrifice, a messenger, a reconciler, and a vessel of the living, loving God.

Like Jesus, we must determine that our lives are not our own, our money is not our own, our reputations are not our own, and even our bodies are not our own. Then when we're confronted with an opportunity to love or serve or support, we won't waver or hesitate or hide. We'll quickly ask, "What would You have me do, Lord? How can I show the Father's love in this situation?"

But for the many times we don't ask the question, "What would Jesus do?" or don't respond to the inner promptings to love another with our actions or words, we must allow the Word of God to be our guide, putting shape and definition to what God's love really looks like:

Turn the other cheek (Matthew 5:39).
Be quick to listen, slow to speak, and slow to get angry (James 1:19).
Take care of widows (1 Timothy 5:3).
Feed the hungry (Romans 12:20).
Do not judge others (Matthew 7:1).
Love your enemies (Luke 6:35).
Wives, submit to your husbands (Colossians 3:18; Ephesians 5:22).
Husbands, love your wives (Ephesians 5:25).
Do not exasperate your children (Ephesians 6:4).

14-21

Visit prisoners, care for the sick, and clothe the needy
(Matthew 25:36).

Practice hospitality (Romans 12:13).

Reconcile others to God (2 Corinthians 5:17–20).

Restore sinners gently (Galatians 6:1).

Don't go to bed angry (Ephesians 4:26).

Forgive seventy times seven (Luke 18:22).

Love your neighbor as yourself (Luke 10:27).

Be patient (1 Corinthians 13:4; 1 Thessalonians 5:14).

Never tire of doing right (Galatians 6:9).

Endure hardship (2 Timothy 2:3; 4:5).

Be self-controlled (1 Thessalonians 5:6).

Give thanks in all circumstances (1 Thessalonians 5:18).

Be joyful always (1 Thessalonians 5:16).

Don't worry about anything; pray about everything
(Philippians 4:6).

Be content in all things (Philippians 4:12).

Avoid even the hint of sexual immorality (Ephesians 5:3).

Hate evil (Romans 12:9).

Do not repay evil with evil (Romans 12:17).

Don't put your hope in wealth (1 Timothy 6:17).

Turn away from godless chatter (1 Timothy 6:20;
2 Timothy 2:16).

Do not be ashamed to testify about your Lord
(Romans 1:16; 2 Timothy 1:12).

Live a life worthy of your calling (2 Thessalonians 1:11;
Ephesians 4:1).

Devote yourself to prayer (Colossians 4:2).

Rejoice with those who rejoice (Romans 12:15).

Mourn with those who mourn (Romans 12:15).

Do not lie (Colossians 3:9).

DAY 19 CHALLENGE

What I am going to say next is incredibly sincere. If you will read the Word of God every day—and truly become familiar with it and allow it to enter your heart—your heart will *burn* to please God. Your love for others will be ignited! His passion will become your passion. You will think big, you will be bold, and you will love outrageously!

Begin today by highlighting at least three of the verses in this chapter that cause you to stretch. Then take the time to write an action plan that includes where, when, and how much it might cost you to do each of them.

Give yourself a deadline for completing this assignment. When you've finished the tough ones, do the same for some of those that are more natural for you to do.

14-21

DAY 20:
DREAM BIG

One of my spiritual heroes is Henrietta Mears. As I mentioned earlier in this book, the talk she gave at a teacher's training conference was the catalyst that started the 1947 Fellowship of the Burning Heart.

Mears was born in 1890 in Fargo, North Dakota. After spending years as a schoolteacher, she worked in the Christian Education department at First Presbyterian Church in Hollywood from 1928 until her death in 1963. In addition to her church work, she founded a publishing company, now called Gospel Light Publications, and she established a large conference center in California called Forest Home Christian Conference Center, both of which are still impacting lives in the twenty-first century.

Colleen Townsend Evans is a former student of Henrietta Mears's and speaks highly of her ministry. She said that she and her husband, Louis H. Evans Jr., "learned there, from her example, to be bold before God, to ask great things on God's behalf and to do spiritual warfare from a bent-knee position."[41]

One of the defining traits of Mears's life was that she challenged everyone she encountered to dream big and to do big things for God. She said that a person who "lays small plans will measure its accomplishments accordingly."[42]

Leadership was Mears's theme, and during her years at First Presbyterian Church in Hollywood, more than four hundred students heard God's call and turned their energies to full-time Christian work in the United States and throughout the world. Yet she inspired all of her students to be ministers in whatever profession they chose, making a difference for Christ in every life they encountered.

As *Dream Big*, the biography of her life, says, "Absolute surrender to the influence of the Holy Spirit was a cardinal factor both in Henrietta's life and in her training of others."[43]

She taught students how to recognize the Holy Spirit's direction in their lives with simple instruction. She would prompt, "Is there the faintest glimmer of light? It may be ever so small. What is it? Follow it! And as you do God will reveal the rest." She also exhorted youth to "plunge into the deep adventurous waters of faith to prove the promises of God."[44]

Henrietta held to a personal "Ten Commandments," one of which immediately and radically changed the way I treated others. Her seventh commandment was: "I will never let anyone think I am disappointed in him."[45] Implementing this concept in my life was revolutionary! I had used guilt to manipulate many conversations prior to reading her commandment. Henrietta Mears was radical. She was sold out and set apart and sent out. And she called others to be and do the same . . . by example!

One of my favorite quotes of hers that greatly inspires me is this: "If you place people in an atmosphere where they feel close to God and then challenge them with His Word, they will make decisions."[46]

In 1947, Henrietta went overseas and began to sense a move of God in her life as never before. On Tuesday night, June 24, 1947, after returning from Europe, she met with hundreds of young Christian leaders at the campground. She spoke with urgency, calling them to become "expendable" for God, compelling them to ask God what they could do for Him. She challenged them to be difference makers, disciple makers, and to love prayer and the study of the Word of God.

As I have mentioned throughout this book, a few men who had been powerfully moved during Henrietta's talk later found themselves at her cabin door asking for prayer. Bill Bright, Richard Halverson, Louis H. Evans Jr., and Henrietta Mears prayed on and on, for long hours, weeping and confessing sin, "asking God for guidance and seeking the reality and power of the Holy Spirit. Then the fire from heaven fell, for God answered their prayers with a real vision."[47]

At the conclusion of their impromptu prayer meeting, they defined their purpose and developed the written pledge of the Fellowship of the Burning Heart. With an extra measure of God's power, within the next twenty-four hours, they prayerfully planned a conference to be held only two months later.

14-21

They publicized the event and spread the word, sending invitations across America. The eight-day conference would be held at the same conference center where the Fellowship of the Burning Heart was birthed. As the teams went out to invite people to the conference, they also invited people to join the Fellowship.

They began circulating literature, which said, in part:

> God has spoken. The revival has started . . . the Holy Spirit spoke to a small group as they knelt in prayer. . . . He gave them a vision with a plan for world-wide evangelism, filling them with the power of the Spirit in a manner not unlike the experience of the disciples at Pentecost. The Holy Spirit has continued to lead. . . .
>
> There is continued evidence that this revival is the work of the Holy Spirit and not something conjured up in the minds of men. This has been demonstrated by the fact that this experience was followed by personal confession of sins by individuals in great numbers and complete consecration of life on the part of many heretofore lukewarm Christians. Such action must necessarily precede any great religious movement, thereby providing "cleansed vessels" through which the Holy Spirit may work.[48]

Not knowing how many would come, when more than six

hundred people showed up at the conference center that held only five hundred, expectation was in the air.

The event was unscheduled. Speakers had been invited but given no time frames in advance, as the commitment was made from the onset that "the hour-by-hour program would be led by the Spirit of God, and no leader was to speak who had not been singled out by the Spirit working through the entire faculty, chaired by Henrietta Mears."[49]

The first day began with the group congregating in an open-air meeting place called Victory Circle. That entire day was filled with testimonies of how people had been compelled to come to this event.

Then Henrietta slipped away to pray. Realizing that so many lives were ready to make a difference in their world but unprepared to do so, she then spoke to the crowd about sin, confession, forgiveness, and the power of the Holy Spirit. If they would just be truly honest with God and give Him their lives and their hearts—the center of their desires and passions and personality—they could change the world!

Eighty-seven colleges and universities were represented at this first of many events called the College Briefing Conference. Henrietta Mears "encouraged every possible effort to win young men and women on campus to Christ."[50]

Present in every meeting from 1947 to 1949 were public confessions of sin and great calls and commitments for students to surrender their hearts to the Holy Spirit, whatever direction that might take them.

14-21

History records that from this first conference, several organizations were formed and more than four hundred young people answered calls to leadership positions and full-time ministry. Because one woman dared to dream big, her life and legacy continues to impact the world six decades later!

DAY 20 CHALLENGE

There is a dream within your heart that is bigger than you! God is asking you to fulfill it.

Andy Stanley has another word for the dream in your heart that won't go away: *vision*. In his book *Visioneering*, Stanley says, "Vision is a clear mental picture of what could be, fueled by the conviction that it should be. A vision requires an individual who has the courage to act on an idea."[51]

Become a lover of God and a leader for God who reflects the depth of His Word and is filled with the power of His Holy Spirit to change the world!

Begin by identifying your passion, your vision, or your dream—in writing. Ask God to show you what steps to take to move forward. Don't be afraid to dream big!

ablaze with purpose

DAY 21:
ABLAZE WITH PURPOSE

I've shared a little about the series of events in the summer of 2004 that turned my son's entire life upside down and set him ablaze with purpose.

As Jake struggled with finding a post-college direction that fit his personality and passions, my observation was that he wasn't really in touch with God's plans for his life. He was in a more self-centered mode, if you know what I mean.

But the call of God was relentless. In fact, this story begins twenty-seven years ago with the guy Roger asked to be our best man. Several months ago, we received an e-mail from him. He is a fellow youth worker turned inner-city pastor, and he wrote to us about a fabulous organization that combines sports with student ministry in Third World countries and inner cities. They are headquartered in Cleveland—our former hometown.

That type of organization seemed like a great fit for my son's love of sports and teaching, especially as he spent the past two years as an elementary physical education teacher in a small

Christian school. But I knew that if I tried to coordinate the effort with my son, it might not produce positive results.

Yet God continued putting pieces and people into place.

As I mentioned in Day 5, Roger's family set a date for a big reunion just outside of Cleveland. Jake had no intention of going, but we began realizing that if Jake attended the reunion rather than taking the solo vacation to Chile he had planned, he could request an interview with the sports/mission organization while there and also attend a Christian character development conference being held in Michigan a few days later. This opportunity required that a lot of pieces fall together, and Roger and I kept a bit of a distance, knowing our son had to be the one making the decisions.

At the last minute, Jake decided to go to Cleveland. During his interview, God ignited Jake's passion for the sports ministry. He caught the vision both for what the organization was about and what he could bring to the table. They had a position open in Spain, but it was a long shot for Jake. They didn't offer him the job right away but agreed to consider him as a candidate. Jake got really excited about the possibilities, and more importantly, he began feeling and articulating a call on his life!

At the conference in Michigan a few days later, God took Jake a step further and struck him with His purifying fire. Jake came home a different person. I found myself listening to him and wondering who in the world this young man had become! Only a month later, Jake traveled to Spain to interview in the city where he hoped the organization would assign him to work.

Roger and I watched the fire build within our son. One of our greatest joys was observing how oblivious Jake was to the obstacles! He didn't possess all the skills necessary for the job, but he pursued it and applied for it anyway. He was full of a faith that his dad and I hadn't seen in him before. We absolutely knew God was giving him courage, ideas, patience . . . so many traits Jake had never exhibited before.

As things were unfolding, Jake often shared various "impossible" details about this faith-filled adventure, and I quickly realized that if I answered him as a protective mom, or as a previously disgruntled youth worker who knew how difficult it was to raise support, or if I responded with negativity or with discouraging words, I could easily extinguish his fire.

I realized Jake is a dreamer—just like his mother. So I began to pray more and talk less.

Jake called me this morning to tell me, "I got the job! They want me in Spain as soon as I can raise my support."

Knowing my son's love of adventure, I asked, "Are you excited?"

Suddenly, I sensed a hesitation in his bubbly enthusiasm. He said, "I have to write letters and raise all of my support before I can leave to do the work in Spain, and they still want me to leave as soon as possible. There is a real need there . . ." Then he listed the many obstacles that stood in his way. With the push to get the job behind him and the reality of the call on his life now evident, I came alive!

From one dreamer to another, I said, "Jake, this is where

14-21

God shows up! He has asked you to do something big for Him. When things look impossible, that is when God reveals Himself to more people than just you! He is going to meet your needs, Jake. And I'll be happy to help you do whatever you need to get started."

You see, I am well trained!

Jake's experience reminds me of the truths I learned in Henry Blackaby and Claude King's study, *Experiencing God*. Since this handbook exploded onto bookstore shelves in 1990, it has helped countless people connect to God in a more intimate, personal way. In *Experiencing God*, Blackaby and King identified seven practical stages through which all men and women can be in a relationship with God: knowing, loving, hearing, joining, believing, obeying, and experiencing God.

The first four stages remind all of us that God loves and pursues every single one of us! He is a God who wants to be in a relationship with us. He speaks to us, and He wants us to be involved in His work. The beginning stages are exciting, emotionally satisfying, and inviting. So far, so good.

The next stages outlined in *Experiencing God* require that we not only recognize God's voice through our Bible reading, prayer time, circumstances, and the church but that we respond back to God, who speaks to us!

It is in our responses to God where we truly begin experiencing the passion and purpose of our lives! Blackaby and King believe that the fifth stage is where "God's invitation for you to work with Him always leads you to a crisis of belief that requires faith and action."[52]

In other words, if you think that knowing God is all about excitement or that you will never encounter difficulty in your walk with God, think again!

I marvel at how Blackaby and King explain this crisis of belief as a good thing. They say, "God is wanting to reveal Himself to a watching world. He does not call you to get involved just so people can see what you can do. He calls you to an assignment that you cannot do without Him. The assignment will have God-sized dimensions." They warn the reader that this is the very place or stage that "many people miss out on experiencing God's mighty power working through them. If they cannot see exactly how everything can be done, they will not proceed. They want to walk with God by sight. To follow God you will have to walk by faith, and faith always requires action."[53]

Here is the reality. We all want to experience God, but we don't want to . . .

> experience pain or
>> let go of unhealthy relationships or
>>> change our living arrangements or
>>> switch jobs or
>>>> give away our time or money!

Yet, for faith to be real, it requires radical actions on our part.

Blackaby and King call this sixth stage of experiencing

14-21

God—crisis of belief—a "must"! In order to experience God, they suggest that we must make adjustments to our thinking, circumstances, relationships, commitments, actions, and/or beliefs. And they don't pretend that the leap from our old ways to God's new ways will be anything but difficult and life changing.

When you experience a crisis of belief, don't run away or stop because you can't see. Move toward this crisis with actions that require changes in your attitudes, career, relationships, bank account—or in any other way God asks.

Finally, we begin to truly experience God as we trust Him with our lives. On the other side of our faith-filled responses to God are the people at work, home, and school who are watching us. As they observe how God is working in us, *they are also experiencing God!*

So who is the God others are experiencing through us?

I recently received a newsletter from David Wilkerson, pastor of Times Square Church in New York City. He wrote about his concern toward believers, especially ministers, who are growing discouraged to the point of giving up their ministries and struggling to hold on to their marriages! Pastor Wilkerson challenged and encouraged all of us with the words of 1 Thessalonians 1:5–8:

> For when we brought you the Good News, it was not only with words but also with power, for the Holy Spirit gave you full assurance that what we said was true. And you know of our concern for you from the

way we lived when we were with you. So you received the message with joy from the Holy Spirit in spite of the severe suffering it brought you. In this way, you imitated both us and the Lord. As a result, you have become an example to all believers.

If you truly want to experience God, where you feel your heart ablaze and burning brightly and where others see the flame in you, know that it is your unrestrained obedience to His voice and joyful surrender of your life that will most mightily release His power and purpose in you.

When we deeply believe that God loves us,
no matter how difficult or overwhelming our experience
is at the moment,
and we respond by trusting Him enough to do anything
He asks of us,
others will see God working in our lives and be changed
as well!

14-21

This is the experience of a burning heart that will set the rest of the world on fire.

DAY 21 CHALLENGE

The beauty of God's love toward men and women of all generations is that He repeatedly chooses people who are not perfectly skilled, highly educated, efficiently funded, or from the best homes. Yet they experience the supernatural, unexpected, and miracle-working power of God in their lives!

God has His own set of requirements. Are you willing to relocate? Willing to work hard? Willing to wait? Willing to do what He asks of you, even if it isn't sensible? Are you able to recognize His voice? Are you available right now? Are you flexible?

You and I can never look at someone and presume we know God's plan for that person's life. Neither should we discourage anyone from searching after and following God's voice or marching orders. At the same time, we must actively follow after the God who loves and pursues us. To experience God fully and powerfully, our most intimate adviser, friend, coach, and confidant must be God.

Today, fan the flame and fuel the fire of your heart by acknowledging, in writing, His love and pursuit of you. Agree with His Word that says He has a plan for your life. Tell Him you want to be involved in His work and fulfill His plan. Admit that you have great flaws and weaknesses, but because God has chosen you, you will go and do whatever He asks of you!

Ask Him to fill you up to overflowing with an extra measure of His Holy Spirit. Confess any areas of your life that are wrong, troublesome, dead weight . . . or sin.

Today, leave behind any complaints and fears and turn your entire life—body, mind, and will—over to the living, loving God. Now get ready to develop your Burning Heart Contract— and begin the adventure of your lifetime!

PART THREE

YOUR BURNING
HEART CONTRACT

We spent the previous section of the book exploring . . .

the passion in prayer,

the power in purity, and

the call to purpose

that fuels lives that burn for God.

Though we touched on the purpose of a Burning Heart Contract at the beginning of this book, now that we've journeyed this far together, I think it's worth coming back to the question, "Why a contract?" Why not just say, "Okay, God, I commit all of these things to You," and be done with it?

First, my disclaimer: there is nothing magical about signing your name to a Burning Heart Contract. Carrying around a piece of paper with a few lines scribbled on it will not bring the power of heaven down on you. Nor will it cause God's voice to bellow through the air, miraculously voiding out all of the challenges, pain, heartache, and trials that are currently in your life.

A Burning Heart Contract doesn't change or enhance the awesome, available power of God toward us; *it simply acknowledges our response to it!* God's part of the covenant to us is already forever signed, sealed, and delivered through salvation in Jesus

Christ. We do not need God to be more powerful, faithful, loving, committed, or purposeful—He is already all that we need.

A Burning Heart Contract is your response to the living, loving God and what He is asking of you. It is the proof of your pledge to live differently from this moment on.

Therefore, the next step is optional and should be entered into only if you feel called by God to do so. Though it may not be easy or feel comfortable, I believe you will know *without a doubt* if you are being led to enter into a written commitment with God for the rest of your life.

I have made many life-changing decisions, usually alone or with only one other person. But at each point of crisis, I ran toward God and was driven to my knees by His Spirit.

When I was suicidal, something drew me to a church. I didn't know I would find a stranger waiting for me who would offer to pray with me and introduce me to Christ! Yet I have never forgotten that day, August 26, 1976, or the kind janitor. Almost daily, for three months, he mentored me, and when we reconnected again twenty-five years later, I could tell him I still loved and followed God!

When I moved out of the apartment I shared with my live-in boyfriend, I had not read a Bible or heard a sermon. I was compelled to obey the inaudible voice of God asking me to refrain from sexual immorality and wait—in purity—for a man who would love me enough to make a lifelong commitment to me. From that day forward, I stood firm. I waited, and God brought into my life a wonderful man who has respected and loved me for more than twenty-seven years.

When I made the final decision to never have another drink of alcohol, I was on my honeymoon, in a hotel room with my husband (of one day!). On the plane heading to Miami, the flight attendant, who knew nothing of my alcoholic background, gave us a bottle of champagne. He was just being celebratory. I hadn't had a drink in more than a year, and no alcohol was served at our wedding. But for some reason, we opened that bottle in our hotel room and made a toast! My husband left the room temporarily and I drank half of the bottle in the next few minutes. I lost my sobriety that day. That was the turning point when I understood I will always be an alcoholic and I can never, ever drink. I asked my husband if he would never drink again with me. As a couple we decided to abstain from alcohol for the rest of our lives! We made a verbal contract that we have kept for more than twenty-seven years. And every wedding anniversary, we also celebrate our sobriety date!

When I made the decision to pray one hour a day for the rest of my life, I was one of many in a conference room. I don't know how that message affected anyone else, but I refused to let the sin of prayerlessness rule my life any longer. After the message I sat there, refusing to leave the room until God met me and changed me. When I wasn't sure what to do next, a woman offered to pray with me. I prayed words of radical commitment that no one asked me to pray, yet I knew God Himself was calling me to do so. Almost twenty years later, when I (for the first time since then) saw the woman who prayed with me, I enthusiastically reminded her of the time she witnessed my commitment to prayer that had significantly changed the rest of my life. She had no idea how important that prayer and her accountability were in the first few days of my commitment!

When I decided to send a letter to twenty-five family members, friends, and co-workers, asking them to forgive me for my out-of-control emotions, it was because the Holy Spirit had convinced me that my anger was very hurtful to others and, more importantly, displayed a serious lack of holiness in my life. During one Fourth of July weekend, God helped me write the letter and identify the people to whom to send it. Then He gave me the courage to send the letter! In the letter, I not only asked forgiveness of each person, but I also asked them to keep me accountable to "never lose control of my emotions at any time." This decision has had an enormous effect on my life.

Good intentions and guilt have never proven powerful enough to truly change me. I've needed a more radical approach —a resolve, often in writing—to successfully change my life. And each time I made a life-altering decision, I sought accountability so that going back was never an option. I needed to drive a stake in the ground and make a stand . . . forever.

The Burning Heart Contract is a marker on your spiritual journey where *you* can drive a stake in the ground and acknowledge the moment of decision, the time in your history when you decided to change for good. With this contract, you are saying, "Lord, You are worthy of my total devotion, and I will live a life that honors You and displays Your faithfulness for others to see. I commit to this adventure with You, and I am committed to doing this for the rest of my life."

The contract is not about making your life easier; it is about making it simpler. Honestly, there is something exhausting about constantly deciding and redeciding who you are or what you believe. If you present yourself as one person with co-workers or school buddies, another person with your family, and yet another person when you walk through the church doors, the internal battle will gnaw at your spirit as you constantly assess, *Who am I, and how should I behave in this particular situation?*

My prayer is that your Burning Heart Contract will become a declaration that you are sold out and set apart to just one Person and that you are being sent out with one purpose. Your contract not only states your intentions for today but sets before you a vision of where you're heading. Let it be a tangible document that allows you to look back at any time and remember how you responded to God's great love with all of your heart, mind, and body.

LEAVE A LEGACY

Whether you refer to it tomorrow, next month, next year, or forty years from now, your commitment to God will remain relevant and inspiring if you daily fuel your fire.

The Burning Heart Contract reflects a life that is driven,

compelled, and consumed with being available and usable for God's work. Recognize, like Bill Bright, Henrietta Mears, and the others in the Fellowship of the Burning Heart of 1947, that fulfilling the terms of your written pledge to God is a lifetime adventure you need never outgrow no matter how successful, famous, or effective you become.

Whether you realize it or not, each of you is creating a legacy for those who come behind you. Imagine the treasure you might one day leave as your children or grandchildren sift through the mementos of your life and come across a worn-out piece of paper that describes your love for God. They will read your handwritten words of passion, purity, and purpose in Christ. And as they consider the evidence of your life, they will understand the call of being sold out and set apart for the Almighty God, who knows and loves them as well.

The week after my father died, I received a letter from the executive director of Cleveland Youth for Christ, the organization where my father worked for thirteen years. The letter said, "I don't know if you knew that your dad signed this, but each staff member is asked to sign a document declaring that they personally know Jesus and have given their lives to Him. I thought it would bring you and your family great comfort to see your dad's declaration of faith." I had no idea my dad had signed this paper. Though we knew my dad loved the Lord and gave His life to Him, it was very meaningful to see it in his own writing.

The signed document was a wonderful and powerful example that a man who lived a difficult life was willing, at the age of sixty-six, to declare his love for God and to spend the last thirteen years of his life in youth ministry as a bookkeeper. Dad loved and served his Lord more in the last thirteen years of his life than in the first sixty-six years!

BLAST THE TRUMPETS

The book of 2 Chronicles contains an insightful story of people who made a joyful commitment to God after discovering the privilege of committing themselves to Him. King Asa became the king of Judah after the death of his father. The account of his reign begins in 2 Chronicles 14:2 with the words, "Asa did what was pleasing and good in the sight of the LORD his God."

But King Asa was a proud and self-reliant man. Although he knew God and claimed to serve Him, Asa was missing something in his relationship with the Lord. Unlike King David, who understood the love of God like that of a dear friend, Asa was prone to call on God only when facing a powerful army in battle. But God knew how to reach Asa's heart.

Scripture tells us that God brought a significant victory for Asa's army on the battlefield. After the king and his men returned home, the Holy Spirit sent a message to Asa through a prophet named Azariah.

"The LORD will stay with you as long as you stay with him!" the prophet told Asa. "Whenever you seek him, you will find him. But if you abandon him, he will abandon you. For a long time Israel was without the true God, without a priest to teach them, and without the Law to instruct them. But whenever they were in trouble and turned to the LORD, the God of Israel, and sought him out, they found him" (2 Chronicles 15:2–4).

Azariah finished God's message to King Asa by saying, "Be strong and courageous, for your work will be rewarded" (v. 7).

The experience of hearing the voice of God breathed into his life through the mouth of a prophet instantly set Asa's heart on fire. The Bible says he "took courage" and destroyed the idols in his land and repaired the neglected altar at the Lord's temple (v. 8). King Asa called together the people of Judah and inspired them to worship God in Jerusalem.

And then the most remarkable thing happened among the people. "They entered into a covenant to seek the LORD, the God of their ancestors, with all their heart and soul. . . . They shouted out their oath of loyalty to the LORD with trumpets blaring and rams' horns sounding. All in Judah were happy about this covenant, for they had entered into it with all their heart. They earnestly sought after God, and they found him" (vv. 12–15).

The message to Asa is the same for us today: if we will seek the Lord, *we will find Him.* "The eyes of the LORD search the whole earth in order to strengthen those whose hearts are fully committed to him" (2 Chronicles 16:9).

Your Burning Heart Contract—this *covenant*—is your

chance to shout joyfully to God, "I will spend the rest of my life seeking You in all that I do and with everything I have. My time is Yours. My mind, body, and spirit are Yours. My dreams, hopes, past, and future are Yours. Oh God, my heart is Yours!"

Blast the trumpets, shout for joy! In other words, make sure others see and hear it; let them know you're excited about something new in your life!

If you are ready to sign up for the greatest adventure of your life, then this is a moment that can change your life, redirect your future, and consume your soul.

HOW TO WRITE A BURNING HEART CONTRACT

The three components of your Burning Heart contract include a written commitment to . . .

prayer and the Word every day of your life,

purity and holiness in every area of your life, and

purposeful living.

What becomes clearly evident once you commit to prayer, purity, and purpose is that the success of each component is completely dependent upon the other.

IGNITE YOUR PASSION

I am convinced that changed hearts and Spirit-filled lives are birthed and sustained through prayer. I am also confident that studying the writings of the great prayer warriors throughout history has something to do with my conviction. Therefore, before you consider making a personal commitment to spend time with God, I want to share some of their incredibly profound thoughts with you:

O. Hallesby wrote, "A child of God can grieve Jesus in no worse way than to neglect prayer."[1]

Wesley Duewel wrote in *Mighty Prevailing Prayer*, "Many neglect prayer to such an extent that their spiritual life gradually dies out. Those who are careless about prayer show that they are careless about other spiritual things. They are rarely ready to be used by God. Prayerlessness means unavailability to God—a sin against God's love."[2]

Hudson Taylor asked, "Should we not do well to suspend our present operations and give ourselves to humiliation and prayer for nothing less than to be filled with the Spirit, and [be] made channels through which He shall work with resistless power? Souls are perishing now for lack of this power."[3]

Oswald Chambers wrote, "Prayer does not equip us for greater works; it is the greater work."[4]

In *Celebration of Discipline*, Richard Foster wrote, "To pray is to change. Prayer is the central avenue God uses to transform us. If we are unwilling to change, we will abandon prayer as a noticeable characteristic of our lives. But when we pray, God slowly and graciously reveals to us our evasive actions and sets us free from them."[5]

Because I have spent one hour a day with God for more than twenty years—during days of intense ministry, as a busy parent and committed spouse, and in spite of my easily distracted personality—I know that I am not asking something of you, no matter your age or stage in life, that cannot be done. Of course, it will most likely mean that you reevaluate your priorities, reschedule or revise less important commitments, or even force yourself to do something initially that you find difficult to do.

I have two helpful suggestions to get you started.

First, *plan your time with God* one day in advance. Do not presume that for the rest of your life, or for that matter, even for the next month, you will be able to meet Him at the same time every day. As your life changes with more or less responsibility, you are free to make your non-negotiable appointment with the King during the first uninterrupted hour of your day . . . whether you are at home, on a business trip, or on vacation.

I am convinced—especially because of my own success in this area—that planning your appointment with God *one day in advance* is the practical key to sustaining a lifelong commitment to spending time with Him. Set aside a specific amount of time for each day, knowing that it can always be increased.

Second, *have a loosely structured plan* that allows you to talk to God (Praise, Admit, Request, and Thanks) and to listen to God (Listening, Messages, New Testament, Old Testament, Proverbs, and To Do) in writing. Planning is essential for you to keep your Burning Heart Contract.

For more than twenty years, every day, I have used *My Partner Prayer Notebook* with lined pages, and for almost two decades I've used the *Change Your Life Daily Bible*, a 365-day Bible. I have found that these resources continually provide a place for my two-way conversations with God where I am never free to avoid confession and where I am always free to receive instruction from Him!

Prayerfully consider the options and suggestions laid out in the seven days of challenge designed to ignite your passion for God. Determine today what commitments, decisions, and patterns you will embrace in order to keep your internal fire daily ablaze for the living, loving God.

The following commitment is the first of three written statements to transfer to your final contract:

MY HEART BURNS TO GROW MORE PASSIONATELY IN LOVE WITH GOD. I MAKE THE FOLLOWING SPECIFIC COMMITMENT TO SPEND TIME WITH GOD DAILY, BOTH TALKING AND LISTENING TO HIM . . .

PURIFY YOUR LIFE

In the written pledge of the Fellowship of the Burning Heart of 1947, the signers determined to stand for holiness, right where they lived. They made a commitment to purity—chastity for singles or fidelity for married couples—and sobriety.

The frame of reference for this portion of the Burning Heart Contract can be summarized in two words: *godliness* or *worldliness*. Begin by asking yourself, "Which word more accurately describes my life?"

If you desire to be set apart for God, I encourage you to make specific, rather than general, decisions for every area of your life.

Having lived a portion of my young adult life consumed by worldliness, I know firsthand its powerful draw. As a young woman, I fell very hard in love with the world. I indulged in out-of-control drinking, drug use, and sex, and I was addicted to each of them in a very short amount of time. In the process, I damaged my dreams, my reputation, and most of my relationships.

So when I see believers actively, heartily, and joyously taking part in those things that look like the world, I simply can't reconcile the issue. When believers run after the things the world often likes to do in darkness, I believe there is no other result than to diminish the power of God in their lives.

If you desire to be set apart for God, it means that holiness—which is generally defined as moral blamelessness—is an overriding characteristic of your life. If you decide to be set apart for God, I encourage you to make a lifestyle choice of holiness, now and forever.

Therefore, whether you are single or married, I believe that the purity God desires for your life must start at your core, with your desires (heart) and motives (thoughts), and it will permeate your words and actions. Second Peter 1:3–9 says:

> By his divine power, God has given us everything we need for living a godly life. We have received all of this by coming to know him, the one who called us to himself by means of his marvelous glory and excellence. And because of his glory and excellence, he has given us great and precious promises. These are the promises that enable you to share his divine nature and escape the world's corruption caused by human desires.
>
> In view of all this, make every effort to respond to God's promises. Supplement your faith with a generous provision of moral excellence, and moral excellence

with knowledge, and knowledge with self-control, and self-control with patient endurance, and patient endurance with godliness, and godliness with brotherly affection, and brotherly affection with love for everyone.

The more you grow like this, the more you will become productive and useful in your knowledge of our Lord Jesus Christ. But those who fail to develop in this way are shortsighted or blind, forgetting that they have been cleansed from their old sins.

Society is allowing greater freedom with sex, drugs and alcohol use, and even profanity. And the walls of the church cannot promise protection or immunization from such things. Even Christians are addicted to everything from television, food, pills, and pornography. Divorce is rampant, affairs are commonplace, and excess is the norm.

If, as a believer, you find yourself struggling to decide which habits hurt other people, that is an honorable question to ask. But on a deeper level, the better question might be, "Does this habit help, glorify, edify, strengthen, or bring honor to me, others, or God?"

But this is *your* contract.

Here are some practical options and suggestions to consider:

I suggest that you ask God to give you *His* holiness standards for your life. (It might mean that you stop now to look up verses in the Bible that discuss holiness and purity and then make this a matter of prayer and fasting before moving forward.) When deciding how you might live a pure, holy, and set-apart life for God, consider not only your desires or what you think you can handle—but the weaknesses of those around you as well.

In the realm of sobriety, my personal encouragement for anyone in leadership is to consider refraining from drinking alcohol in public because of the abuse that pervades every age group of our society. Those who have a family history of alcoholism are wise to embrace complete abstinence as a model for other family members. Parents should carefully and prayerfully consider the use of alcohol, even in their home, in their duty as role models. Bottom line: alcohol is a substance that alters our mood and chemical makeup. It is addictive both through genetics and through continued use. And under the influence of alcohol, we are prone to do things that we would not otherwise do—and that often cross sexual, moral, and legal boundaries.

Perhaps you might ask yourself, "If I removed alcohol completely from my life, would my life reflect more of God? Would I have greater effectiveness in my life and ministry? Would this be an encouragement or hindrance to others? Would it be a worthy or worthless sacrifice?"

In the area of sexual purity, be specific. If you are married, define your commitment to sexual purity as including everything from your fantasies to your boundaries with the opposite sex. If single, you should define "purity boundaries" for touching the opposite sex both in casual dating relationships all the way through engagement. As a counselor, my husband has used one blanket statement for every age group—elementary kids through engaged adults: "Just don't touch each other's private parts!" This might be a clearly defined boundary that you can embrace until marriage.

Finally, if you are young, 1 Timothy 4:12 says, "Don't let anyone think less of you because you are young. Be an example to all believers in what you say, in the way you live, in your love, your faith, and your purity." As a student, your impact is great. Consider the weight of your decisions not only as they impact others, young or old, but also as they impact your future.

The greatest motivation of those with burning hearts is to glorify God and be completely usable by Him. Second Timothy 2:21 makes it clear that purity is a prerequisite to achieving God's purpose for your life: "If you keep yourself pure, you will be a special utensil for honorable use. Your life will be clean, and you will be ready for the Master to use you for every good work."

I encourage you to define a pledge of purity that includes practical and personal decisions about your *mind* and *body*.

MY HEART BURNS FOR GOD'S HOLY SPIRIT TO FILL ME AND MAKE ME PURE. AS AN ACT OF LOVE AND DEVOTION TO GOD, AND IN RESPONSE TO HIS CALL THAT I BE PURE AND HOLY, I COMMIT MY MIND AND BODY TO . . .

_____

_____

··

FULFILL YOUR PURPOSE

A. B. Simpson said, "God chooses people He can depend upon. God is looking for people on whom He can place the weight of His entire love, power, and faithful promises. And His engines are strong enough to pull any weight we may attach to them. Unfortunately, the cable we fasten to the engine is often too weak to handle the weight of our prayers. Therefore God continues to train and discipline us in His school of stability and certainty in the life of faith. May we learn our lessons well and then stand firm."[6]

A passionate and purified heart is sent out with a purpose to draw, lead, and introduce others to God. The first question of the Westminster Catechism asks, "What is the chief end of man?" The response: "Man's chief end is to glorify God and to enjoy him forever."

A life that is impassioned through prayer and empowered by purity reflects God in a most brilliant way. It is appealing, contagious, and humble. It radiates with a fire and enthusiasm because of its convictions.

The apostle Paul reminded Timothy of the all-encompassing power available to a life that is fully devoted and committed in every area to the living, loving God. He said, "Hold on to the pattern of wholesome teaching you learned from me—a pattern shaped by the faith and love that you have in Christ Jesus. Through the power of the Holy Spirit who lives within us, carefully guard the previous truth that has been entrusted to you" (2 Timothy 1:13–14).

The 1947 Fellowship of the Burning Heart pledge committed each participant to leading at least one person each year to Christ.

The desire for others to know and love God only took a few years before it caused Bill Bright to write yet another contract, one that was even more specific. Bill and his wife, Vonette, dedicated their marriage and earthly possessions to the Lord. In 1951, they founded an organization called Campus Crusade for Christ, now present worldwide, which has reached hundreds of millions of people in 181 countries with the good news of Jesus Christ.

In their later pledge, Bill and Vonette Bright stated that the purpose of every man and woman is to glorify God. In the most tangible way they could articulate, they determined to bring glory to God by fulfilling the Great Commission (Matthew 28:19–20) one person at a time. Bill Bright later said, "Frankly, I've never known a happy Christian who was not involved in the Great Commission."[7]

I believe that being available to God to lead at least one person each year into a personal relationship with God is a very honorable and serious commitment. Those of us with the spiritual gift of evangelism might find that reaching out to one person a year with the goal of introducing him or her to Christ is easy and natural. Others of us with different spiritual gifts and more introverted personalities might find that sharing our faith with others is intimidating. Yet I believe that no matter our spiritual gift, God absolutely calls each of us to be a part of the Great Commission.

As you consider this section of your Burning Heart Contract, I have two suggestions: one is personal to you and the other is general to all believers.

First, spiritual gifts are given to every believer by God Himself. The use of our gifts is an act of worship. When God gives a particular gift to us, He knows—from before all time—when and where we will walk through life. He gives us these gifts for a purpose. If you have never identified your spiritual gift, you must not hesitate one day longer to do so. Every believer has a spiritual gift. The New Testament details these gifts, but in this twenty-first century, manuals, books, and even on-line spiritual gifts tests abound! Do not neglect to use the gift God has given you to bring Him glory. Your gift is designed to fit with a team of others and complete the team! As Paul wrote to Timothy, "This is why I remind you to fan into flames the spiritual gift God gave you when I laid my hands on you" (2 Timothy 1:6).

If you do not know your spiritual gift or you are not actively using it, then you must begin immediately to do so. Your written commitment should reflect this.

Second, I believe that when we become Christians, we are immediately called into ministry (2 Corinthians 5:17–20). Each one of us is given a responsibility: to reconcile others to God, just as we have been reconciled! Therefore, on a daily basis, from the moment you get out of bed until you hop back into bed at night, your life is *intended* to bring the power and person of God to your family members, neighbors, co-workers, acquaintances, even strangers and passersby.

Take God with you everywhere you go. If and when God puts a thought in your mind or prompts you by His Holy Spirit to say or do something, act on it! Be His ambassador.

I think of it like this: I try taking each person I encounter one step closer to God each time we meet. If it is only once, I do my best to present the living, loving God to that person through my words, smile, patience, encouragement, respect, or tip.

I encourage you to define your life's purpose by making a very personal but tangible decision that can be pursued daily!

My heart burns to fulfill God's purpose in and through my life. Through my spiritual gifts and my call as a believer to reconcile others to God, my tangible commitment to fulfilling God's purpose in life includes . . .

_____

_____

_____

_____

CAN I GET A WITNESS?

I also included a place in this contract for a witness to sign. I encourage you to exchange your contact information with another person who will be your accountability partner for at least three years. Though this time frame might sound excessive, I figure if you're with me this far, you're in it all the way. So, to maximize your potential for success, I suggest that you connect daily with your partner for the first ninety days of your contract (by e-mail or phone), and then once a week for three months, and then once a month (or six more times) during the first year. Then, continue checking in once a month, or twelve times, during the second year, and four times during the third year. After that, your commitment should be solid, and you can determine how to continue in your accountability relationship.

I also encourage you to start a Burning Hearts Club with any other friends who are on the same journey to be sold out, set apart, and sent out! Meet weekly, bring your contracts, and stay accountable to each other through prayer and confession! And at every anniversary, celebrate!

YOUR BURNING HEART CONTRACT

IGNITE YOUR PASSION

MY HEART BURNS TO GROW MORE PASSIONATELY IN LOVE WITH GOD. I MAKE THE FOLLOWING SPECIFIC COMMITMENT TO SPEND TIME WITH GOD DAILY, BOTH TALKING AND LISTENING TO HIM . . .

PURIFY YOUR LIFE

MY HEART BURNS FOR GOD'S HOLY SPIRIT TO FILL ME AND MAKE ME PURE. AS AN ACT OF LOVE AND DEVOTION TO GOD, AND IN RESPONSE TO HIS CALL THAT I BE PURE AND HOLY, I COMMIT MY MIND AND BODY TO . . .

FULFILL YOUR PURPOSE

MY HEART BURNS TO FULFILL GOD'S PURPOSE IN AND
THROUGH MY LIFE. THROUGH MY SPIRITUAL GIFTS AND
MY CALL AS A BELIEVER TO RECONCILE OTHERS TO GOD, MY
TANGIBLE COMMITMENT TO FULFILLING GOD'S PURPOSE
IN LIFE INCLUDES . . .

_____

_____

_____

_____

_____

_____

_____

_____

_____

_____

_____

_____

_____

_____

_____

Signed: _____ Date: _____

Witness: _____

PART ONE: WHAT IS A BURNING HEART?

1. O. Hallesby, *Prayer* (Minneapolis: Augsburg, 1931), 39.
2. Leonard Ravenhill, *Revival Praying* (Minneapolis: Bethany House, 1962), 105.
3. Ibid., 60.
4. *My Partner Prayer Notebook* (Newport Beach, Calif.: Becky Tirabassi Change Your Life, Inc, 2004 rev. ed.).
5. Michael Richardson, *Amazing Faith: The Authorized Biography of Bill Bright* (Colorado Springs: Waterbrook, 2000).
6. Ibid., 37–38.

PART TWO: A 21-DAY ADVENTURE IN PASSION, PURITY, AND PURPOSE

1. Ros Rinker, *Prayer: Conversing with God* (Grand Rapids: Zondervan, 1959), 23
2. James Reimann, ed., *Streams in the Desert* (Grand Rapids: Zondervan, 1997), 294–95.
3. Quoted in Rueben P. Job and Norman Shawchuck, *A Guide to Prayer for Ministers and Other Servants* (Nashville: The Upper Room, 1983), 380.
4. Ibid.
5. Roger Steer, *George Muller: Delighted in God* (Colorado Springs: Shaw, 2000 rev. ed.).
6. Job and Shawchuck, *A Guide to Prayer for Ministers and Other Servants*, 368.
7. Helmut Thielicke, *Encounters with Spurgeon* (Grand Rapids: Baker, 1963).
8. Andrew Murray, *The Inner Life* (Grand Rapids: Zondervan, 1950), 12.

9. *Change Your Life Daily Bible* (Wheaton, Ill.: Tyndale, 1999).

10. Wesley Duewel, *Ablaze for God* (Grand Rapids: Zondervan, 1989), 211–12.

11. Jodie Berndt, *Praying the Scriptures for Your Children* (Grand Rapids: Zondervan, 2001).

12. Reimann, ed., *Streams in the Desert*, 236.

13. Ravenhill, *Revival Praying*, 105, 124

14. Jerry Bridges, *The Pursuit of Holiness* (Colorado Springs: NavPress, 1978), 102.

15. Reimann, ed., *Streams in the Desert*, 407.

16. Oswald Chambers, *The Psychology of Redemption*, (Ft Washington, Penn.: Christian Literature Crusade, 1930), 13.

17. Duewel, *Ablaze for God*, 76, emphasis in original.

18. Ibid., 26.

19. Graham, *The Holy Spirit* (Waco: Word, 1978), 14–15.

20. Duewel, *Ablaze for God*, 278.

21. Graham, *The Holy Spirit*, 108.

22. J. I. Packer, *Knowing God* (Downers Grove, Ill.: InterVarsity, 1993), 211.

23. Hannah Whitall Smith, *One Christian's Secret to a Happy Life* (Springdale, Ill.: Whitaker, 1983), 99–102.

24. Richardson, *Amazing Faith: The Authorized Biography of Bill Bright*, 93.

25. Ibid.

26. Thielicke, *Encounters with Spurgeon*, 94.

27. Richard Foster, *Freedom of Simplicity* (San Francisco: Harper SanFrancisco, 1998), 105.

28. Spence and Exell, eds., *The Pulpit Commentary*, Vol. II (Peabody, Mass.: Hendrickson, 1985), 187.

29. Ibid.

30. Thielicke, *Encounters with Spurgeon*, 72, emphasis in original.

31. Ibid., 93.

32. Bridges, *Pursuit of Holiness*, 19.

33. Graham, *The Holy Spirit*, 94.

34. Luis Palau, *Heart After God* (Sisters, Ore.: Multnomah, 1982).

35. Bridges, *Pursuit of Holiness*, 39.

36. From the Leadership Academy Web site, hosted by Dr. Tim Elmore, 2004, http://www.growingleaders.com/courses/academy.html

37. Rick Warren, *The Purpose Driven Life* (Grand Rapids: Zondervan, 2002), 234, 236.

38. Job and Shawchuck, *A Guide to Prayer for Ministers and Other Servants*, 305.

39. Ibid., 306.

40. Duewel, *Ablaze for God*, 109.

41. Earl O. Rowe, ed., *Dream Big: The Henrietta Mears Story* (Ventura, Calif.: Regal, 1990), 21.

42. Ibid.

43. Ibid., 20.

44. Ibid., 223.

45. Ibid., 281.

46. Richardson, *Amazing Faith*, 26.

47. Rowe, ed., *Dream Big*, 227.

48. Ibid., 286.

49. Ibid., 292.

50. Ibid., 295.

51. Andy Stanley, *Visioneering* (Sisters, Ore.: Multnomah, 1999), 18.

52. Henry T. Blackaby and Claude V. King, *Experiencing God* (Nashville: Broadman & Holman, 1994), 36.

53. Ibid., 36–37.

PART THREE: YOUR BURNING HEART CONTRACT

1. O. Hallesby, *Prayer* (Minneapolis: Augsburg, 1931), 48–49.

2. Wesley Duewel, *Mighty Prevailing Prayer* (Grand Rapids: Francis Asbury, 1990), 30.

3. Duewel, *Ablaze for God*, 306.

4. Oswald Chambers, *My Utmost for His Highest*, October 17.

5. Richard Foster, *Celebration of Discipline* (New York: HarperCollins, 1978), 33.

6. Reimann, ed., *Streams in the Desert*, 426.

7. Richardson, *Amazing Faith: The Authorized Biography of Bill Bright*, 202.

CONTACT INFORMATION

To contact Becky Tirabassi

or

for more information on

THE BURNING HEART CONTRACT,

companion resources,

or Burning Heart Events,

please call or write or e-mail:

800-444-6189

Burning Hearts

P.O. Box 10926

Newport Beach, CA 92658

www.theburningheartcontract.com

letters@theburningheartcontract.com